A GUIDE TO
SUCCESSFUL SEARCHES
FOR COLLEGE PERSONNEL:
☐ *Policies, Procedures,*
☐ *and Legal Issues*

By John M. Higgins
    Patricia A. Hollander

The Higher Education Administration Series
Edited by Donald D. Gehring and D. Parker Young

COLLEGE ADMINISTRATION PUBLICATIONS, INC.

© 1987 College Administration Publications, Inc.,
All rights reserved. Published 1987
Printed in the United States of America
91 90 89 88 87   5 4 3 2 1

Library of Congress Cataloging in Publication Data

Higgins, John M., 1929—
    A guide to successful searches for college personnel:

    (The Higher education administration series)
    1. College teachers—United States—Selection and
appointment.   2. College administrators—United States—
Selection and appointment.   3. Employee selection—Law
and legislation—United States.   I. Hollander, Patricia A.
II. Title.   III. Series.
LB2835.25.H54   1987   378'.12'0683   86-32725
ISBN 0-912557-07-9

The views expressed in this book are those of the individual
authors and are not necessarily those of College Administration
Publications, Inc.

This publication is designed to provide accurate and
authoritative information in regard to the subject matter
covered. It is sold with the understanding that the publisher is
not engaged in rendering legal, accounting or other professional
service. If legal advice or other expert assistance is required, the
services of a competent professional person should be sought.

*—from a Declaration of Principles jointly adopted by a committee of the
American Bar Association and a committee of publishers.*

ii

Table of Contents

Table of Charts, Illustrations & Samples

Foreword

The search for administrative and faculty personnel is an extremely important function today for all colleges and universities. Full awareness of the legal parameters created by the various civil rights laws, and the regulations pursuant thereto, which mandate specific treatment and prohibit certain actions, is absolutely imperative when searches are undertaken.

The expense of a search also requires that administrators plan well to ensure that the best applicants are attracted to the openings and that the institution is properly presented and looks its best. One way for this to be accomplished is to have a well-planned search procedure from the beginning.

In this monograph the authors have laid out a step-by-step plan to assist administrators with every aspect of the search procedure. The sample forms, letters, and checklists each conform to the legal guidelines established by both statutes and current court decisions.

This monograph should be a most helpful tool for administrators in the planning and execution of the entire search procedure. It will also be a valuable aid for everyone who serves on a search committee or is involved in anyway with the search.

DDG
DPY
Series Editors
January, 1987

About the Authors

JOHN M. HIGGINS, President of Higgins Education Consulting, a private New York firm, has been an Academic Administrator at several institutions including service as Vice President for Academic Affairs at Medaille College, and Academic Dean at both Mansfield University and LaRoche College. He was the first Dean of Teacher Education at the newly established Riverina College for Advanced Education in New South Wales. He has consulted frequently in the area of Adult Education for the Poor and College Curriculum Development. He has also chaired and supervised many Search Committees.

Dr. Higgins received his Ed.D. from the University of Toronto. He has served as a faculty member and administrator in colleges and universities in Australia, Canada and the United States. In 1979, he was a member of the American team that surveyed Egyptian education for the United States Agency for International Development. Dr. Higgins has addressed groups as diverse as the Jamaican Teachers Association, the New South Wales Principals and Infant Mistresses, The Council for the Advancement of Small Colleges and the Pennsylvania Association for Teacher Education.

PATRICIA A. HOLLANDER is an attorney in Buffalo, New York. Since 1972 she has been the General Counsel of the American Association of University Administrators.

Ms. Hollander received her J.D. law degree from St. Louis University and did graduate work at Harvard Law School. At the State University of New York at Buffalo, she served for almost a decade as both an administrator and a faculty member in the School of Management and in the School of Law. In spring 1980, she taught at the University of Virginia's Center for the Study of Higher Education, as Visiting Professor.

Ms. Hollander is the author of *Legal Handbook for Educators*, published in 1978 and co-author of *A Practical Guide to Legal Issues Affecting College Teachers* published in 1985. She is an editor of *The Computer Law Monitor*, a quarterly publication that summarizes in lay language significant court cases concerning computer technology. Her latest book, *Computers In Education: Legal Liabilities and Ethical Issues Concerning Their Use and Misuse*, was published in 1986.

Chapter I

Introduction

The process of selecting faculty members, administrators or staff is not just a plan to add personnel to the college. It is an exercise in public relations, investigation, writing, evaluation and perhaps, is an institutional political action. In addition, the conduct of the parties during the process has legal ramifications.

SEARCH COMMITTEE EDUCATION

Members of the search committee must be educated about basic principles of writing advertisements, affirmative action and equal employment compliance. The committee must also develop communication skills needed to draw out information from candidates and those who recommend candidates.

A good search is time consuming and arduous. It requires being aware of institutional affirmative action policy (or practice if the institution does not have a written policy). One error, depending on the magnitude, may result in institutional embarrassment, administrative reprimand or even lawsuits.

PUBLIC RELATIONS

A search for new personnel is an exercise in public relations. Poorly worded or misleading advertisements, imprecisely written communications, improperly handled interviews, misunderstandings over travel reimbursement are all factors which may reflect adversely on the academic community's perception of the college.

Advertisements for faculty members are usually placed in professional journals or newsletters. Each advertisement may be read by thousands of professionals and may become a part of the process by which a reputation is earned. For example, a few years ago a small midwest college advertised for an instructor in its "college without

1

walls" program—in a prison. This oxymoronic announcement was noted in the Marginalia column of *The Chronicle of Higher Education* with glee, possibly to the mild embarrassment of the writers of the advertisement.

Persistent advertisements of this sort will eventually lead some administrator within the institution to question the competence of the person who writes such copy. Persons who read consistently foolish or inappropriate advertisements may wonder about the competence of the institution itself.

More serious blunders may allow readers to infer sexual, racial, ethnic, religious or economic biases on the part of the advertiser. The resulting anger on the part of persons sensitive to real or imagined biases may cause unfavorable publicity.

On the other hand, well-written, highly informative, yet businesslike advertisements often give the impression that the advertisement represents a well-run institution.

ADVERTISEMENTS

Well written advertisements should help to cut down on applications from persons patently unsuited to the position and encourage applications from those who are qualified. Imprecise advertisements may attract a large number of applications from persons who are unsuited to the position. As each application must be logged, recorded, reviewed and answered, it is far better to save time and money required for application processing by trying to solicit applications only from those whose qualifications are clearly appropriate.

LETTERS

Letters to applicants should be clear and precise in meaning. Many letters sent to applicants and candidates have a legal or quasi legal significance. Letters that set forth position descriptions, qualifications, employment conditions and/or a search and selection timetable may be interpreted by applicants as agreements on both substance and procedures.

All communications with prospective college employees represent the college to a group of applicants and also to any other persons to whom they show the correspondence sent to them. Clearly written, courteous letters give the recipient the message that the search process is legitimate and that the college is well administered.

Unclear messages, discourtesy, failure to acknowledge applications and lack of notification of the results of the search may present the college or department as uncaring, discourteous and, perhaps, administratively inept.

APPLICANTS

Applicants are looking at the college, too. The search is not a one-sided proposition. Even though an announcement may bring scores or hundreds of applications, it is possible that the most highly qualified and attractive candidates will be lost to the institution if all care is not taken in the search process. Applicants have been known to withdraw applications on the basis of written and oral communications from a college.

An illustration of multiple withdrawals from a search conducted by an eastern college took place when the college acknowledged applications by post card. A number of applicants for the position (a vice presidency) felt that this type of reply was egregious to say the least. Not only did they withdraw their applications but they discussed the matter with others in their fields and added or detracted in some manner from the reputation of the advertising college.

INTERVIEWS

It is necessary for all interviews to be planned. The composition of a committee is also important. No member of an interviewing committee should have a conflict of interest or an obvious bias which will jeopardize the committee's recommendations.

Biases or conflicts of interest may become evident during an interview with the committee, or a person being interviewed may perceive a bias. While complaints of bias or prejudice do not usually end up in court or with the college forced to make a financial settlement, such charges do take time to answer and sometimes the most flimsy allegations can cause embarrassment to individuals or to the college.

PURPOSE OF THIS PUBLICATION

It is hoped that this publication will provide some basic guidance to search committees. The charts, letters, timelines and forms are offered as suggestions. They were designed to be adapted to the specific needs of individual colleges.

TERMINOLOGY

The terms used in this monograph that need standard meanings are explained below:

Affirmative Action—Most colleges have had to file plans with federal agencies to assure that persons of either sex, of any race, religion, national origin, handicap or within certain age limits will be given equal consideration for position openings for which they qualify.

College personnel offices that were required to file Affirmative Action Plans are required to maintain statistics on the sex, race, ethnic, age, and handicap composition of the applicant pool. The purpose is to demonstrate that over the long haul, the number of qualified persons employed from these various protected groups is proportional to the number available in the labor pool.

Applicant—This is a person who has completed the application procedure necessary to be considered for a position.

Candidate—An applicant who has satisfied the selection committee that he/she has minimal qualifications for the opening and will remain part of the pool after the second review. He/she may expect to be asked for transcripts and anticipate that persons who know him/her will be contacted for references.

College—This word is used throughout the text to refer to any institution of higher education whether it is called a college, university, institute, conservatory, etc.

Contact Person—This person may not exist as an individual. The duties and functions may be divided among a number of persons but the phrase represents a conglomerate of duties. This is the person or persons who must see that all the administrative functions of the search committee are carried out. A personnel officer, the search committee chairperson or someone else may be designated to carry out these duties.

Initial Screening—The first review of applicants' files takes place after the closing date for applications. The initial screening is a check to see that all requested application materials have been received and that the applicants have the required degrees and other formal requirements for the position. Persons whose files are not complete are "screened out." This is not the part of the process that evaluates candidates in terms of the quality with which he/she has met the requirements of the position.

Letter of Acknowledgement—This is the term used for the letter that tells applicants and referees that their letters and materials have been received.

Major Positions—These are positions within the institution that are advertised as carrying managerial responsibilities in addition to those of teaching, researching or being support personnel. While the term is not often used in the academic world, these persons are supervisors. That is, they are department chairs, deans, directors, vice presidents and provosts.

Most Attractive Candidates—This term is used for candidates who are to be invited to the campus for interviews. These are the last candidates in the search process.

Referee—A person who writes letters of recommendation— references—in behalf of candidates.

4

References—These are letters or telephone assurances that a person who is a candidate has the qualifications being sought by the college. They are written by referees.

Search Committee—this committee is constituted to find suitable persons to recommend for specific positions. It conducts the search—the process by which persons are sought to fill positions. The search committee refines the position description and the criteria being demanded, attracts applications and reduces the number of persons being considered to a few or one who is to be recommended for employment. Sometimes the committee is called a Selection Committee or a Search and Screen Committee.

Second Review—After the initial screening, candidates' qualifications are reviewed in greater depth. This is the part of the search that looks for quality and superior achievement within the listed qualifications. At this point, an applicant may be telephoned for additional information.

Short List—After the second review, a list of persons still under review is made. These persons are now candidates and will be investigated rigorously.

LEGAL CONCERNS

Procedures, practices and actions of administrators and of members of a search committee and others involved in the recruitment of faculty and staff for a college or university have the potential for exposing to legal liability the institution as well as individuals personally.

Examples of Legal Complaints

A number of legal complaints have been filed based on allegations of breach of contract, discrimination, or defamation. For example, charges have been made alleging that certain promises were made regarding terms of employment but were not kept, that there was discrimination resulting from job qualifications that did not fit the job description, that the lack of a response or a poorly written response to a job applicant was misleading or discriminatory, that personal interviews were discriminatory and harassing, or that the final job offer meant one thing to the candidate and another to the institution.

Institutional and Individual Liability

When mistakes are made in the course of a search, the institution may be liable for awards of damages and loss of public funding. Individuals, too, may be exposed to personal liability if they act unlawfully outside the scope of their institutional employment.

Preventive Law

Many legal complications may be avoided by prior establishment of search procedures that are clear, appropriate, fair and followed.

The suggestions of sound procedures and preventive legal measures in this monograph are meant to alert administrators, search committee members and others to some of the problems that generally are preventable.

Chapter II

Organizing for the Search

SUPERVISOR

The supervisor is the first figure to emerge on the stage for the search process. This is the person who has the authority to make an offer of employment, or carry the final recommendation of the successful candidate to a higher officer if necessary.

It is the supervisor who will appoint the chairperson of the search committee, confer with the chairperson about the appointment of committee members and, ultimately, accept or reject the recommendations of that committee. The supervisor has at least the following duties:

1. Informs all officers involved that a search is to be conducted. This includes the appropriate academic or support departments and the personnel office.
2. Appoints a chairperson of the search committee.
3. Reviews and agrees to a list of committee members as presented by the chairperson.
4. Meets with the search committee to give it its charge along with any other specific instructions.
5. Assists the search committee with writing the specific position description, including qualifications, duties and responsibilities of the position. The supervisor assists by arranging conferences with the appropriate consultants—academic departments, administrators and other concerned parties.
6. Approves the position description.
7. Outlines the dimensions of the search:
   a. budget for the search;
   b. advertisements—where and when to place;

c. duties of the contact person—division of duties if they are to be divided among chairperson, personnel officer and/or others;

d. desired timetable with significant milestones for completion of search;

e. provisions for secretarial/clerical support;

f. explains any special institutional concerns;

g. outlines necessary record-keeping procedures;

h. describes relationships between the committee and personnel office.

8. Schedules regular appointments for chairperson or committee for discussion of progress or problems.

9. Approves expenses to be incurred for activities of committee including type of mailings to be used (bulk, individual, parcel services, etc.), consultant or other personnel costs, costs of interviewing, advertising and similar matters.

10. Reviews records of applicants rejected after initial screening and second review.

11. Reviews short list.

12. Reviews plans for interviewing.

13. Accepts or rejects recommendations for appointment made by search committee.

14. Assures that an offer is made to the successful candidate in writing.

15. Assures that all interview expenses are paid and that letters are sent advising unsuccessful candidates of the results of the search.

While the supervisor does not have to watch over the shoulders of the search committee and may delegate some of the responsibilities above, he/she is responsible if any fundamental errors or mistakes take place during the search process.

Together with the chairperson and the search committee members, the supervisor conducts the Institutional Survey.

INSTITUTIONAL SURVEY FOR SEARCH COMMITTEE

1. Is there a written policy that covers all phases of faculty/administration/staff selection?

2. Is there a collective bargaining agreement that affects the manner in which searches are authorized, conducted and concluded?

3. How are members of the search committee chosen?

4. To whom does the search committee report?

5. Who is the contact person and how is he/she chosen?

6. If the contact person is not from the personnel office, who is responsible for:

a. receiving application;

b. responding to applications and inquiries;

c. requesting further information from applicants;

d. requesting written references;

e. arranging interviews;

f. notifying unsuccessful applicants.

7. How will letters and memoranda be processed? (is a word processor or memory typewriter available to the search committee?)

8. How much clerical/secretarial time has been allocated for the search?

9. What is the institutional policy on expenses incurred by candidates in order to attend interviews?

10. What is the college policy on expenses incurred by members of the search committee who transport candidates from airport to hotel and who may have meals with them?

11. What information about possible rank and salary may the search committee share with applicants?

12. How many candidates are to be recommended for the open position?

13. Should the search committee recommend rank and salary to the supervisor?

14. Who makes an offer to the candidate?

15. How long will it be after the interviews before a candidate is notified as to whether he/she has been successful?

CHAIRPERSON OF SEARCH COMMITTEE

Normally, the first person to be selected for the search committee is the chairperson. The chairperson often is the head of the unit to which the selected person will report. For example, the chairperson of an academic department may head the search committee for a faculty member for his/her department; a vice president or his/her designee may head a committee searching for a dean; a dean or his/her designee may head a search committee seeking an assistant or associate dean and a president may appoint the head of a committee seeking a vice president.

ROLE OF THE SEARCH COMMITTEE CHAIRPERSON

1. Convenes and chairs search committee meetings.

2. Receives completed applications from contact person and provides receipt for applications to the contact person.

3. Duplicates and distributes application materials to search committee members.

4. Informs contact person when applicants have been eliminated from the search at each step.

5. Assigns telephone calls to referees to search committee members.

6. Arranges conference calls between search committee members and candidates.
7. Together with the contact person, arranges travel and accommodation for the interviews.
8. Schedules visits and interviews with the help of the contact person.
9. Distributes and collects all evaluation and observation forms· to all parties involved in interview procedures.
10. Convenes search committee meeting to identify candidates to be recommended.
11. Advises supervisor of the persons being recommended for position by search committee.
12. Maintains minutes of all meetings of the search committee.
13. Returns applicant files to contact person.
14. Monitors all activities of search committee.

MEMBERS OF THE SEARCH COMMITTEE

The supervisor and the search committee chairperson usually confer as to who will be represented on the search committee.

The search committee should have members who have legitimate interests in the selection process. For example, in the selection of a faculty member, it is important to have on the search committee a number of persons in the discipline subject area and who will be colleagues. For administrative positions, persons who will be subordinates, peers or superiors of the person selected should serve on the search committee. Where the dean of a school is being sought, it is usual to have subject matter specialists as well as prospective peers and supervisors.

It is not unusual to have outside members on the search committee. A committee searching for a person with practical experience in the business world might have a well-known business man or woman or an executive on the committee. If the open position is particularly prestigious, there might be a nationally known figure on the search committee.

Colleges with special needs or considerations might appoint persons to the search committee for a variety of reasons. For instance, a small college which prides itself on individual attention to students might want a person from student services, learning services or other important areas on the committee.

POSSIBLE SEARCH COMMITTEE CONFIGURATIONS
Selection Committee for
Instructor/Assistant Professor, Business Education
Membership:
1. three members form the Department of Business;

2. one member from a department deeply involved with the Business Education Program (Business Administration, Education, English, etc.);
3. one member from the Office of Student Affairs;
4. two students.

Selection Committee for
Dean of the School of Education

Membership:
1. three chairpersons from departments within the School of Education;
2. two senior professors from Education;
3. two junior professors from Education;
4. one member from the professional staff or the Office of the Vice President for Academic Affairs;
5. two senior students.

Selection Committee for
Director of Admissions

Membership:
1. one member from the professional staff of the vice president or dean to whom Admissions will report;
2. one Admissions counselor;
3. one or two representatives from the Personnel Office;
4. one representative from the Office of Financial Assistance;
5. one lower division student;
6. one upper division student.

Student Members of the Search Committee

Many colleges include students among the members of the search committee. The student members are chosen through a variety of mechanisms. Some students are appointed on the basis of the recommendations of members of the search committee who have already been chosen.

Sometimes the student government association is asked to name possible members or provide a list of nominations from which student members will be appointed to the search committee.

Non Acceptable Members

There are persons who should not be part of some search committees. For example, persons with obvious bias against persons of the opposite sex, racial groups, the handicapped and those over a certain age, as well as particular personality characteristics, may be more harmful to the search committee than they are helpful. Also, persons who may be interested in maintaining some political advantages to themselves or their groups, by the selection of a potential ally or supporter, should be avoided.

ROLE OF SEARCH COMMITTEE MEMBERS

Search committee members:

1. set a timetable for each search procedure;
2. formulate the position description;
3. determine criteria for the position;
4. select newspapers and journals in which advertisements appear;
5. write advertisements for newspapers and journals, and the Notice of Vacancy;
6. review applications to determine if the applicants meet the advertised qualifications;
7. develop lists of questions to ask referees by telephone;
8. make telephone calls to referees as assigned by chair and make reports to the entire committee;
9. participate in initial and second screening of candidates;
10. take part in conference calls to candidates;
11. assist chair with travel accommodations and interviewing schedules;
12. participate in observing demonstration class or seminar and formal interview;
13. complete evaluation forms for candidates' demonstration classes or seminars and for the formal interview;
14. participate in final evaluation and formulation of recommendation to supervisor;
15. attend all meetings and maintain appropriate confidentiality about search committee proceedings.

CONTACT PERSON

The contact person is the individual who responds to applicants' inquiries, arranges interviews and informs applicants about the results of the search. The contact person may or may not be a member of the search committee.

Hopefully, the duties of the contact person can be given to one individual. However, if necessary, these duties may be divided among more than one person with the chairperson assuring that the duties are carried out.

In many institutions the contact person may be a personnel officer. In other colleges a department chairman or an administrator may be the contact person.

It is not unusual for some conflict to arise between the personnel department and academic departments about who the contact person should be. Personnel is concerned with the administration and recording of affirmative action and equal employment opportunity policies, and it is necessary that the personnel department has access to certain kinds of information in order to monitor the process. Academic departments and administrators are concerned with getting information about an individual's scholarship, teaching or administrative abilities and interpersonal skills.

While the personnel department must be concerned with the legalities, courtesies and policies of hiring, the academic, support and administrative units and departments must live with the results of the search. Fortunately, it is possible to satisfy the legitimate concerns of all parties. Several arrangements are possible.

1. The contact person may be a personnel officer performing all the duties of a contact person but not sitting on the search committee. He/she receives instructions about the content of letters and other matters which are of concern to the search committee. He/she confers frequently with the search committee chairperson.

2. The chairperson of the search committee also may be the contact person. Then, when answering an initial inquiry or application, he/she may include a request for completion of affirmative action/equal employment opportunity forms in the letter of acknowledgement.

The normal practice is for the required personnel information (the form) to be sent directly to the affirmative action officer and not to the search committee.

An analysis of recent issues of the *Chronicle of Higher Education* reveals that approximately 10% of the employment advertisements directed job applicants to apply to the personnel officer, while 80% provided the name of a faculty member or administrator as the person to whom the applications should be addressed. The remaining 10% gave a variety of different instructions for applying, including sending applications to board of trustee members and to outside consultants.

As advertisements often bring literally hundreds of responses, the contact person must have the resources to fulfill his/her responsibilities. If the individual given the responsibilities is not from the personnel department (which presumably is fully staffed for searches) there must be adequate clerical and professional assistance. It would not be unreasonable, if the contact person is a faculty member, to provide release time for the conduct of the search.

In addition to clerical assistance, the contact person must have an outside telephone line. It might even be desirable for the outside telephone line to have the capacity to handle conference calls with candidates and referees.

A system for maintaining files on applicants is most important. For each candidate there should be a file containing the initial applica-

13

tion, additional application materials, written recommendations, records of telephone calls made, notes of telephone conversations, decisions made by the search committee at each stage of the search, interview records, and copies of all correspondence between the institution and the applicant/candidates.

ROLE OF CONTACT PERSON

The contact person:
1. Places advertisements.
2. Is named in advertisement as the person to whom applications are sent.
3. Acknowledges applications and sends Special Data Form, college and community information, Notice of Vacancy.
4. Holds applications until all requested materials are received.
5. Gives completed applications to chair of search committee. Gets receipt for applications from chair.
6. Informs unsuccessful applicants after initial screening.
7. Requests written recommendations for candidates.
8. Informs unsuccessful candidate after second screening.
9. Makes necessary arrangements for travel, accommodations, interviews for candidates invited to campus.
10. Conducts exit interview.
11. Informs unsuccessful finalists.
12. Monitors process throughout to assure that Affirmative Action and Equal Employment practices are followed.

SEARCH COMMITTEE FUNCTION AND SIZE

Ideally, a search committee should be as small as possible, yet large enough to include as many legitimate interests as possible. It must be remembered that it takes time to meet as often as a search committee will find necessary. The more members, the more difficult it is to have everyone present for the meetings, all of which are important.

Search committees function differently in the cases of faculty, administrative and staff searches. When searching for a faculty member, the committee may present a dean with only one name. However, when searching for an administrator, the supervisor often prefers to have the names of three to five persons from whom to chose.

Whether there is a difference in the results of the search process (nominating one person or several), the essential ingredients for finding a person to recommend remains the same.

DEVELOPING THE POSITION DESCRIPTION AND IDENTIFYING THE CRITERIA FOR THE POSITION

Usually, the department or unit for which the search is being conducted meets with the search committee to decide on the position description and the criteria for selection. Persons who are invited to participate in development of the position description and the identification of the criteria may include faculty members in the department affected and others with whom the selected individual may have to deal. If, for example, a physical education faculty member is also to coach a ball team, the head coach should help develop the position description and identify the criteria for the position. In the case of a search for a dean of an academic unit, faculty members, other deans, and supervisors of the deans should be provided with an opportunity to help develop the position description and identify the criteria.

It is quite true that many colleges have detailed position descriptions on file setting forth duties and authority of faculty members, administrators and staff, but the input of many interested parties can be added to a basic outline available in the college personnel files.

It is also true that many colleges do not have specific descriptions for many positions. In such cases, the search committee is well advised to seek a consensus from the interested parties before proceeding with the next step of the search. Once a consensus seems to be settled, the supervisor's agreement for the position description and criteria should be obtained.

The position description should include an outline of all duties and expectations. The list of criteria or qualifications may include professional, personal and public considerations. Some of these considerations may be:

1. degrees required or deemed important—what is the minimal acceptable degree or configuration of degrees along with other qualifications?
2. what experience is required—teaching, research, practical and other?
3. what scholarly accomplishments—publications, presentations—are necessary?
4. what personal qualities are important?

EXAMPLES OF CRITERIA FOR PARTICULAR POSITIONS

Degrees Required:

What degrees or configuration of degrees and other qualifications are necessary?
   a. M.B.A. and C.P.A. required
   b. Ph.D. and membership in A.P.A. important
   c. Doctorate and eligibility for California Community College Chief Administration Certificate
   d. M.S. in Engineering and M.S. in Computer Information Science
   e. Licensure

CRITERIA WORK SHEET

Position _____

Department _____

Ideal	Acceptable Criteria (to be used for advertisements)

Educational

1. _____   _____
2. _____   _____
3. _____   _____
4. _____   _____

Experience

1. _____   _____
2. _____   _____
3. _____   _____
4. _____   _____
5. _____   _____
6. _____   _____
7. _____   _____

Publications

1. _____   _____
2. _____   _____
3. _____   _____
4. _____   _____
5. _____   _____

Personal

1. _____   _____
2. _____   _____
3. _____   _____
4. _____   _____
5. _____   _____

Other

1. _____   _____
2. _____   _____
3. _____   _____
4. _____   _____
5. _____   _____
6. _____   _____

Experience

How many years in what particular capacity?

    a. Ed.D. with five years public school teaching at the elementary level

    b. A minimum of five years of progressively responsible planning, policy-making and administrative experience at an institution of higher education.

    c. Evidence of an interest in working with students on research projects

    d. A record of significant accomplishment in research, scholarship or entrepreneurial experience

    e. A record of at least five years in academic or business administration

    f. A minimum of three years community college experience

Publications and Research

What is required?

    a. A record of scholarship and publications essential

    b. Must be nationally recognized in his/her field

Personal Qualifications

What commitments and additional abilities are required?

    a. The ability to articulate the goals and mission of the college internally and externally

    b. A strong commitment to the Community College concept is essential

    c. The post requires commitment to the ideals of liberal arts education in a women's college

    d. A strong commitment to ideals of Christian education is essential

    e. The ability and stamina to raise funds from both public and private sources is necessary

    f. A full commitment to Catholic education in the Jesuit tradition is expected

---

TIMETABLE

Often a search committee underestimates the length of time it takes to conduct a search. Periods of waiting are unavoidable. Advertisements do not appear overnight and sometimes it may be a month or more before an advertisement will appear in an appropriate journal.

There are also periods of time allowed for receipt of applications and the many documents that will be required eventually. Telephone inquiries must be made and the persons who are being called are not always available to answer calls. Delays are part of the process and must be anticipated.

A search, conducted properly, takes months and each search has variables which may lengthen the process. A few of the issues that may determine the timeline for the search are:

1. Who needs to be notified once a search has been approved by the appropriate supervisor?

In some instances, a collective bargaining agreement may provide that before a search may be advertised, the union must be notified that a vacancy exists and that a search is about to be conducted.

In some state-supported colleges, a central administration office may have to be notified or even approve. Any delays in starting the search because of these or other factors should be taken into account.

2. How long will it take before an advertisement will appear?

Professional journals may not be published monthly and, therefore, it may be several months after formulating the advertisement before it will appear in the desired publication.

Most professional journals will provide a potential advertiser with a schedule listing deadline dates for placing advertising.

An advertisement in a local newspaper may appear within a day or two after the newspaper receives the advertisement. However, if a display advertisement is desired in a particular section of the newspaper, it may be necessary to wait weeks until the particular space is available.

3. How long must the advertisement run in order to meet affirmative action and equal opportunity employment guidelines?

Often an institution will have a policy specifying how many times an advertisement must be run and in which media. This will be a minimum number of times in one or more specified journals. There may also be a policy stating how long an interval is required between the first appearance of an advertisement and the closing date for acceptance of applications. If such a policy exists, it will vary from one college to another and, perhaps, from one category of position to another within the same institution. The length of the interval for a faculty position may vary from three weeks to three months, while that for a vice president or other major position may be from two to six months or longer.

Once as many factors as possible have been considered, the search committee can determine a reasonable timetable.

Unfortunately, timetables are not set in stone. In addition to factors mentioned above that delay searches, there are other situations that might cause delay. Sometimes an insufficient number of applications for a position may be received by the date for closing. If this occurs, a search committee may have to rethink its advertising and reopen the search, rearranging the timetable. The use of a different medium may also be considered for advertising.

In the sample timetable that follows, please note that over four months has been allowed for the search—not a great deal of time if the search is to be done well. If any of the conditions are upset, this particular search may have to be reopened with the hope of finding a suitable person for the following January.

SAMPLE SEARCH PROCESS TIMELINE

Position: **Instructor/Assistant/Associate—Japanese History**

February 15 - 17	Chair and Search Committee chosen
February 21 - 24	Committee meeting — Position Criteria clarified, Advertisement and Notice of Vacancy formulated
February 24 - 28	(1) Mailing list for Notice of Vacancy constructed (2) Advertisement placed in *Chronicle of Higher Education* to appear March 19, 26
March 19 - April 25	(1) Applications received by Contact Person (2) Replies sent to applicants along with Special Data Form
May 15	All completed applications given to Chair, Search Committee by Contact Person
May 16 - 17	Initial Screening by Search Committee
May 20	Contact Person notifies unsuccessful candidates including those whose applications are incomplete
May 21 - 23	Second Review by Search Committee
May 25	Eliminated applicants notified by Contact Person
May 26 - 30	Candidates telephoned, Transcripts and References requested
May 31 - June 4	Referees telephoned
June 6	Committee constructs Short List
June 10	Interviews arranged by Chairman or Contact Person after notifying Supervisor
June 30	Committee recommends candidate for appointment
July 5	Offer made by authorized person
July 12	Offer accepted or rejected

Once the position description, criteria and timetable have been established, the search committee must proceed with attracting applicants for the position.

LEGAL CONCERNS

Lack of Legal Authority to Act

It is essential that all parties understand the scope of authority they have. It must be made clear who has the legal authority to bind the institution. For instance, the written policies of the institution should be consulted and followed with regard to who has the legal authority to authorize a search and who has the authority to make an offer to a candidate. Sometimes, oral representations are made to a candidate by members of a search committee or others lacking authority to make such representations. When a candidate mistakenly relies on such representations, a misunderstanding may result that leads to a lawsuit.

Unclear Position Descriptions and Qualifications

Written position descriptions and written criteria for making selections among candidates are necessary. They inform both the searchers and the applicants of the yardsticks against which applicants will be measured. Adherence to explicit job descriptions and criteria may assist in defending against allegations of job discrimination or unequal treatment.

A position description for a faculty, staff or administrative position should be accurate. It should state the duties and responsibilities, whether it is a tenured, continuing or non-tenured/at-will position, what the salary or salary range is and what the term of the appointment is.

Position qualifications or criteria for selection should be directly related to the position description. Included should be requirements such as: formal education, licensure, experience, scholarly research, publications, and referees. If tests are contemplated for matters such as competency, truthfulness, drugs or AIDS, there should be prior consultation with legal counsel.

Unclear Search Procedures

The search procedure to be followed and the role of members of the search committee, faculty, administrators and staff support personnel should be clarified and explained to all concerned.

The time frame for the search also should be stated.

Chapter III

Advertising

The purpose of an advertisement is to reach the largest possible audience of persons qualified for and interested in the position. Therefore, it is essential to place the advertisement in newspapers, journals, and newsletters that reach the desired audience. The person placing the advertisement must ask several questions before deciding on the medium to be used for advertising:

1. Whom are we seeking.
2. What publication does the kind of person being sought read?
3. Where do we place an advertisement that will attract the applicants we seek and at the same time meet college policies and guidelines?

NEWSPAPERS AND JOURNALS

If the person being sought is likely to be one who is currently employed in a college or is completing graduate study, the Education Advertising Section in the Sunday edition of the *New York Times* or the *Chronicle of Higher Education* might be appropriate and effective. However, if it is thought that the person being sought is not currently in academe and, therefore, is not aware of these two publications, it may be necessary to advertise in other print media.

If a college is seeking a person in the business or accounting area, it might be productive to place an advertisement in one of the regional editions of the *Wall Street Journal,* the *National Business Employment Weekly* or a regional or local business newspaper.

A search committee should seek advice from persons in the particular discipline or administrative area who know appropriate journals in which to advertise. In the event that the committee is not satisfied with the journals it knows, or wishes to locate additional journals in which to advertise, the committee may wish to consult *Ulbrich's*

International Periodicals Review which is found in most larger libraries. It lists thousands of journals, and their addresses, in many fields. The journals may be contacted for information about cost and deadline dates for the receipt of advertisements.

Large city newspapers often are appropriate places to place advertisements. Display advertisements for technical positions placed in the appropriate section of the newspaper can be most effective.

Classified advertisements can also be effective if placed under the right caption. For example, a classified ad may catch the eye of more readers if placed under the caption *Business Instructor* rather than under *Instructor* or *Teacher*. A person looking for a position in Business or accounting is more likely to be drawn to an ad where the first word is one with which he/she is familiar. Entry level and academic support position advertisements often are effective when placed in local newspapers or the *Chronicle of Higher Education*.

By local newspaper it is not meant just the newspaper in the city nearest to the college. Papers in any metropolitan area are included. As an example, if a college in Nebraska wanted a faculty member in technology, it might be quite appropriate to place an advertisement in local newspapers in geographical areas where "hi-tech" industries are in a decline. There may be many persons in this location with advanced degrees, presently unemployed, who would be most interested in a teaching or research position in a college in Nebraska. Thus, advertisements in Boston, San Francisco or Houston newspapers might bring a good number of applications from persons well suited to a position in Nebraska.

Major administrator positions often gain attention when placed in the education section of the Sunday *New York Times* or the *Chronicle of Higher Education*.

There are also a number of publications that specialize in circulation to women and minority groups. The *Affirmative Action Register* (8356 Olive Boulevard, St Louis, MO 63132) advertises itself as "The only nationally distributed all recruitment publication directed to females, minorities and handicapped." *Black Issues in Higher Education* (4002 University Drive, Fairfax, VA 22030) also carries advertisements for college personnel. Both of these publications carry advertisements for many positions at different levels of responsibility.

The advantage of newspaper and journal advertisements is that these publications have large circulations often targeted to the populations desired by the advertiser. In the case of newspapers, they are published frequently, so an advertisement that is unsuccessful one day may be highly successful in attracting applications the next day or week.

Advertising in the large or nationally circulated publications also demonstrates that the advertiser is meeting one aspect of Affirmative

Action. It is argued that by placing advertisements in mass circulation publications, persons from both sexes and all racial, religious, ethnic, age groups, and the handicapped have the same opportunity to see the advertisement and apply for the position.

Print media advertisements may have a major disadvantage, however. They can be *expensive*. If a college were to place an advertisement in one local newspaper, plus Sunday edition of the *New York Times, Black Issues in Education* and *The Affirmative Action Register*, the costs could run to thousands of dollars. While this expense may be necessary and justifiable for some positions, it is hard to justify it for institutions with modest resources or for an institution with many searches to conduct.

Again, the range of advertisements depends on whom the advertiser wishes to contact. If it is essential that the position notice reach persons in higher education of both sexes and minority groups, it may be necessary to advertise in a number of publications. Some institutions attempt to hold down costs by combining all position vacancies in one advertisement, usually a display ad. The college then is relieved of the expense of numerous advertisements, each containing the same information about the college. However, in display ads individual positions often are not described in detail, and combination position advertisements placed in dissimilar publications simply may not be appropriate.

NOTICE OF VACANCY

Newspaper and journal advertisements are necessary. However, as the number of advertisements that are placed may be limited by the advertising budget and may not reach the persons being sought, they should be supplemented by a Notice of Vacancy Form. These forms when completed are duplicated inexpensively and are sent to college placement services, academic graduate departments, academic deans, admissions officers, department heads and acquaintances. For major positions, some colleges go so far as to have the Notice of Vacancy sent to every academic vice president or college president in the country.

The Notice of Vacancy can be distributed for the cost of a postage stamp and can be targeted as carefully as the search committee wishes.

The Notice of Vacancy usually is a quite detailed description of the position and the institution. As such, it can be included in the information sent to applicants who applied as the result of print media advertising.

Recently, a college seeking an instructor in Computer Information Sciences was not successful in attracting the candidates it wanted. The college sent a Notice of Vacancy to 275 graduate departments of Computer Science (names and addresses found in the *Peterson Graduate Guide for Mathematics*) along with a similar notice to the placement offices of each of the 275 colleges. Bulk mailing was used so that the cost of postage was reduced to a few cents per letter plus clerical time and stationery. (Some bulk mailings may take considerable time to arrange the bundles as the post office requires. If additional clerical time must be paid, it might be less expensive to send all the letters by first class mail.) The bulk mailing replies were greater in quantity and quality than were the replies to the advertisements in the various publications. However, replies were not forthcoming as rapidly because the announcement of the vacancy had to filter through the bureaucracy of the 275 institutions until they became known to graduate students.

BLACK ROCK UNIVERSITY
Buffalo, NY 14200
NOTICE OF VACANCY

Position: Media Communications

Rank: Instructor / Assistant Professor

Duties: To teach undergraduate courses in theory, and to supervise interns. Service on university and departmental committees required as is student advising.

Qualifications: A doctorate in Communications is preferred. However, a master's degree with five years in the media industry will be acceptable.

Application Procedure: Send application with a cover letter addressing the qualifications to:
Director of Personnel
Black Rock University, Buffalo, NY 14200

Black Rock University is a multi-purpose institution with a student population of 2,000, located in the near suburbs of Buffalo, New York. The attractions of the Great Lakes, the numerous cultural events and organizations make this an excellent city in which to teach and live. Buffalo has the lowest housing cost of any large city in the United States. The student body is approximately 40% minority group, 67% female and 67% over the age of twenty-five.

Rank and salary will be based on qualifications.

BRU actively seeks applications from women and members of minority groups.

Development of Mailing List

In order for the Notice of Vacancy to be effective, it is necessary for the search committee to develop a mailing list. An excellent source for the development of such a list is the *Peterson Graduate Guides* (Princeton, NJ). This is a series of graduate guides that list university graduate departments and include the names of chairpersons of the departments. As the guides are published annually, it is presumed that the names and addresses are up-to-date.

Placement Services

There are several kinds of placement services:

1. Many professional associations have placement or referral services. The subject area associations often have listings of openings and may provide room for interviewing at annual conventions. Again, the subject matter specialists on the search committee should be aware of this. For senior positions, professional organizations, such as the American Association for Higher Education, maintain a placement office and are particularly interested in placing female and minority group individuals in major positions.

2. Most colleges maintain placement services for graduates. Some will even send a prospective employer files of persons who seem to fit specified position qualifications. It is then up to the prospective employer to send a copy of the Notice of Vacancy to the identified individuals.

   Other college placement offices will post vacancies in their offices or list them in newsletters sent to those who are registered with the service. The person registered, in turn, contacts the advertiser.

3. Commercial faculty placement agencies often list vacancies. These agencies have files on persons who are seeking teaching positions. The agencies charge either the institution or successful applicants a fee for the service. Usually they are useful only in locating prospective faculty members, rarely administrators or staff.

4. So-called "head hunters" or executive search agencies help to locate senior college officials. Colleges pay a fee—usually a rather substantial proportion of the first year's compensation of the placed person. These agencies advertise vacancies, screen applicants, and recommend a small number of applicants to the searching college. Each agency works in a different manner and it is necessary to contact each one to determine the service offered and the costs.

   Any large metropolitan newspaper will contain advertisements from executive search companies. Their ads usually are those which state "no fee charged" or "employer pays fee."

   The normal precaution of contacting the Better Business Bureau about local executive search companies should be observed. Also, if such assistance is sought, the person responsible for contracting with head hunters should ask for a list of companies for

25

January 13, 1986

PERSONAL & CONFIDENTIAL

Dr. John W. Black
Chairman - Board of Trustees
Black Rock University
Black Rock, Minnesota

Dear Dr. Black:

It was a pleasure meeting with you on December 12, 1985, to discuss your objective to recruit a President for Black Rock University. We welcome the opportunity to provide your institution assistance in this most important activity. Our approach to providing this assistance is described in the following paragraphs.

As I previously stated, we are uniquely qualified to provide this recruiting assistance. Our consultants have served a wide variety of colleges and universities both public and private throughout the United States. We at PA always work confidentially and as an extention of the search committee of the university. We believe that our approach ensuring confidentiality enables the best and the brightest candidates to be considered without compromising their present positions. We also believe that this will result in increased effectiveness for the university by ensuring that the quality of candidates considered is of the highest.

REQUIREMENTS

In providing our assistance we ask the university to describe the details of the environment in which the position will function. Based on this information we would propose a specification which outlines the responsibilities of this position and the background requirements and experience that you are seeking. After review by you, we would use the specification in our contacts with sources and candidates.

METHODS

We believe that the assignment would require a full range of candidate identification methods, including research, sourcing inquiries among business people with relevant knowledge, search of our files, and extensive use of our network of consultants and contacts. We will develop a Prime Target list for your review to indicate the organizations that we would include in our research.

26

To assess interested candidates prior to your meeting them, we would rely on evaluation interviews and on thorough background inquiries and reference checks. The latter method is especially important because it would give us a longitudinal view of ability, personal behavior, and professional performance. For those candidates that we refer to you, we would provide you with written reports that summarize their achievements and contain our evaluation of them.

Attracting preferred candidates would require special effort and sensitivity, because candidates of the quality you seek have a variety of attractive alternatives. PA would be prepared to assist in maintaining effective communications with candidates and in conducting any necessary negotiation.

GEOGRAPHIC SCOPE

The recruitment area will include the entire United States.

TIME SCHEDULE

We would generally plan for you to begin considering candidates who meet your qualifications within six weeks. Thereafter, the time schedule would probably depend more on your place in evaluating candidates than on our ability to find and attract qualified people. We see no reason why the project should not be concluded within three months. Maximum speed, consistent with high quality results, would be in the interest of all concerned.

PROFESSIONAL FEES

Our standard charge is one-third of the first year's compensation, including any probable bonus, for anyone you hire whom we have identified and evaluated for you. We also charge for our expenses including any specialized research. We bill our professional fee in three equal parts: one at the beginning of the assignment, and one at the end of the first two months, if it should take that long.

You, of course, would have the right to cancel the assignment at any time after the first month. In that case, your only obligation would be for our accrued fees and expenses. If a candidate comes to your attention from some other source during the course of the engagement, we understand that you would refer that person to us for evaluation in comparison to the range of alternatives we expect to develop.

We would be happy to meet with you and your colleagues to discuss in more detail our capabilities and approach to providing assistance to Black Rock University recruiting. I will telephone you next week to determine the most appropriate schedule for such a meeting.

Yours very truly,

Bernard E. Brooks

Bernard E. Brooks
Vice President
University

BEB:aah
Enclosure(s)

27

whom successful searches have been conducted and should check with those companies about the quality of the services they received.

For purposes of the college search, a professional service specializing in seeking experienced college personnel is usually best. However, some colleges seek persons with commercial or industrial experience for chief executive positions. In such a case an executive search group specializing in business administrators might fulfill the expectations of the college. (*See letter, pps. 26 &27*)

5. It is becoming more common for colleges to employ an outside consultant for the search. Advertisements have been noted where the instructions are for readers to send their applications to an outside consultant. The outside consultant then does the initial screening or even the second review and forwards records to the college along with his/her recommendation for persons to be interviewed by the college. The outside consultant may also sit as an ex-officio member of the search committee during interviews.

Developing the Advertisement

The advertisement may be very general or very specific in content. Sometimes, in a faculty search, most of the current members of a given department may be generalists and therefore may be able to adjust their teaching assignments to the strengths and interests of an incoming faculty member. On the other hand, an institution or department may have very specific needs. The advertisement should state them. A clear description of duties and qualifications is important in either instance.

There is a middle ground. Some advertisements may list specific courses which applicants should be prepared to teach. While it is important to list the courses, it is usually wise to add "and other assignments to be determined by the college." This phrase gives the college some latitude in assignments after employing the successful candidate.

A brief description of the college is also important. With over 3,200 colleges in the United States, it is not reasonable to expect an applicant to have detailed knowledge about a particular institution. Therefore, it is important to list some of the characteristics of the college in the advertisement.

Applicants are attracted to different types of institutions. They want to know if the college is located in a rural or urban area, what kind of student population the college attracts, how large/small it is, how many faculty members there are, how far it is to the nearest city and what academic specialties are stressed.

Naming a closing date for receipt of the application is also important for most positions. The closing date allows for an orderly termination for receipt of applications. The search committee can deal with what has been received, and reject applications received after that date.

Occasionally, it is difficult to determine whether an advertisement will bring a sufficient number of applications. Perhaps the field is one where applicants are expected to be few, or the advertiser simply does not know what kind of a response to expect. In such a case, the closing date might be stated as "Applications will be received until the position is filled."

Space, budget, and college policy permitting, the following items should be considered in constructing an advertisement:

A. Position Description
  1. Title
  2. Duties to be fulfilled (teaching, advertising, special committees, program development, supervising, etc.)
  3. Research and publications
  4. Fund raising
  5. Public relations activities
  6. Supervisory activities
  7. Budgetary responsibilities
  8. Person (title) to whom position reports
  9. Grant writing
  10. Other

B. Position Requirements
  1. Formal education (Ph.D., D.B.A., M.B.A., M.L.A., etc.)
  2. Experience (teaching, research, publications, business, social agencies, etc.)
  3. Licensure

C. Position Conditions
  1. Rank
  2. Salary range
  3. Tenure/non tenure, replacement position, temporary, etc.
  4. Contract
  5. Travel required
  6. Institutional support (travel, research, etc.)
  7. Religious affiliation or commitment required
  8. Other conditions

D. The College
  1. Location
  2. Student population and characteristics

3. Mission of the college
4. Graduate/undergraduate
5. Residential/commuter
6. Other

  E. Application Information
    1. Person to whom application is to be sent
    2. Materials to be sent with application
    3. Closing date

It may be that, for various reasons, an institution does not wish to address each of the above items. If all items are not placed in the advertisement, perhaps in order to lower the advertising cost, those items omitted may be put in the Notice of Vacancy which will go out in the packet sent to those who apply as a result of seeing the advertisement. However, the advertisement should contain all the descriptive elements that are considered essential.

Encouraging Applicants

To encourage qualified applicants, the advertisement should make it relatively easy and inexpensive for a qualified person to apply.

A significant number of advertisers ask that respondents to advertisements have official transcripts and letters of recommendation sent in support of the initial application. This demand by the advertiser inhibits many persons from applying. It can also make the whole search process unnecessarily complicated.

While a college may receive 200 applications for a given position, it is also not unusual that a serious position hunter will have an equal number of applications out. That applicant may be most reluctant to ask his/her referees to write to a large number of potential employers.

It can also be expensive for an applicant to have official transcripts sent at the beginning of a search process. For example, if an applicant earned each of three degrees in a different institution, it may cost twelve dollars or more for transcripts plus postage, cost of typing, and duplication of vita to complete an initial application which, in effect, is little more than an inquiry. Many highly qualified position seekers avoid applying to colleges that make these demands.

From the point of view of the college, such a demand can be self-defeating: If each of two hundred applicants sends three or more transcripts, three references, and a letter of application, that is a total of seven documents from each individual, or a grand total of 1,400 pieces of material, each one of which is important.

Of the 1,400 pieces of material, 800 must be answered (each application and each recommendation).

This is an enormous job for any office, whereas a request for a cover letter and a copy of the curriculum vita would require responding only to the applicant at this early stage of the process.

While 200 responses to an advertised faculty vacancy is not unusual, advertisements for administrators may bring even more applications. Three hundred applications for a position in a desirable location is not unknown.

To complete the initial step of the search process, with hundreds and probably thousands of documents, increases costs in stationery, postage, and employee time, and almost guarantees clerical problems in smaller and medium size colleges.

It is argued that it is far more efficient to request just a cover letter and a curriculum vita at the initial application state, for it is not unusual to find that only thirty or forty applicants are viable after an initial screening and *before* there is a need for recommendations and transcripts. If requests for references and transcripts are sent to applicants *after* the initial screening, the applicant then is more likely to feel that it is worthwhile to go to the additional expense of having such documents sent.

It is also reasonable to assume that qualified persons for senior positions will be unwilling to submit references at an early stage, being wary of letting potential referees know that they are considering changes of position. It is very likely that the applicant most sought by the advertiser will be the most reluctant to comply with the instructions for applying.

There is a question, too, about the value of written references that are forwarded along with the application at the request of the applicant. They are often from friends whose interest is in helping the applicant-friend. References sent at this time are rarely analytical.

The advertiser should consider well before demanding references with the initial letter from the applicant.

HANDY PHRASES AND SENTENCES TO CONSIDER WHEN CONSTRUCTING ADVERTISEMENTS AND NOTICES OF VACANCY

- transcripts and recommendations need not be submitted in advance but will be required of all finalists
- applicants should send a cover letter relating qualifications to requirements of the position.
- applications will be accepted until the position is filled (*used when few applications are anticipated*)
- names, addresses, and telephone numbers of three persons knowledgeable about the applicant's background and qualifications should be sent with application
- the successful candidate may be expected to teach evenings and off-campus courses.

Applicants often complain that advertisements that are placed in the more popular media—*Chronicle of Higher Education,* and the *New York Times*—are not bona fide. They point to the wording of announcements of recent appointments to support their contention that the results of a search were predetermined. Far too often announcements will read "Jonathan Smith, acting vice president to vice president." or George Custer, acting dean to dean." or "Mary Jenkins, acting Vice President for Student Affairs to Vice President for Student Affairs." To combat the notion that a search is not being made in good faith, some colleges have chosen to add to position advertisements, where appropriate, the phrase "The acting vice president (dean, chairman, etc.) is NOT a candidate for the position."

CHECKLIST FOR ADVERTISEMENTS

	YES	NO	N/A
1. Is the advertisement specific about the position description?	—	—	—
2. Are required qualifications for the position specific enough to discourage the unqualified from applying?	—	—	—
3. For instructional positions, are additional duties (committee work, office hours, research and publication expectations, etc.) noted if important?	—	—	—
4. Is rank noted?	—	—	—
5. Is a salary range noted?	—	—	—
6. Are there any personal qualifications or attributes noted (environmental concerns, foreign language ability, computer literacy, social problem awareness, etc.?)	—	—	—
7. Are tenure, non-tenure, or length of contract noted?	—	—	—
8. Is there any preference for persons of a particular age group, sex, race or personal habits noted?	—	—	—
9. Is there a description of the college and student population?	—	—	—
10. Is there some mention of the community?	—	—	—

EXAMPLES OF ADVERTISEMENTS

A number of advertisements and comments about their content follow. Please note that even though an advertiser may not put in all the information suggested, it may be by design and not default. Some institutions do not want to note a salary range in their advertisements, and other colleges may wish to withhold certain non-essential information for a variety of reasons. Advertisements may also be short to hold down the costs; however this is apt to result in the application and screening of many who would not apply if provided the proper information at the outset.

VICE PRESIDENT FOR STUDENT AFFAIRS
Black Rock University

Black rock is a comprehensive university located five miles from downtown Buffalo, the second largest city in the state of New York. Student enrollment is 2,000 with approximately 40% of the students from minority groups and 67% over the age of twenty-five.

The major areas of responsibility of the Vice President are admissions, registration data distribution, counseling, enrollment management, records, testing, financial aid, veterans services, student services (extra-curricular as well as co-curricular), placement and alumni services, intercollegiate athletics and intercultural affairs.

The candidate we seek should have an earned doctorate from a regionally accredited institution with an emphasis in student personnel services. Related experience in college administration is required.

All material, including a cover letter addressing the qualifications, transcripts and letters of recommendation should be directed to: Director of Personnel, Black Rock University, Buffalo, NY 14200 by July 1, 19--.

Comments on Preceding Advertisement

- Transcripts and references are requested with initial application. This requirement tends to reduce the number of applications.
- The information provided about the college is adequate.
- There is no information about salary or possible rank.

ASSISTANT TO PRESIDENT & EQUAL OPPORTUNITY DIRECTOR
Black Rock University

Black Rock University announces a search for the position of Assistant to the President and Director of Equal Opportunity. The position reports directly to the president and will be filled not later than January 1, 19--.

Apply to: President Hartley Jones
Black Rock University
Buffalo, NY 14200

33

Comments on Preceding Advertisement

- No information is provided about the college.
- There is no indication of salary or possible rank.
- There is no description of the duties of the position.
- There are no instructions for applying for the position.

SPECIAL EDUCATION
Assistant/Associate Professor for Fall, 19--.

Nine month tenure track position. Doctorate in Special Education or Curriculum and Instruction with significant course work in Special Education; a minimum of three years experience teaching special education populations, experience in field supervision; evidence of scholarly/creative productivity and grant development; specialization in elementary language development and English and a second language preferred; teach graduate and undergraduate course in generic special education, educational diagnostics, learning disabilities and/or emotional disturbance, elementary curriculum. Salary and rank based on qualifications, excellent benefits.

Black Rock University is located in an excellent suburb of Buffalo, New York, the second largest city in the state. It has an enrollment of approximately 2,000 with 40% from minority groups. Numerous baccalaureate and master's programs are offered in Education.

Submit letter of application, curriculum vita, transcripts and three letters of reference by June 30 to: J.P. Smith, Chair, Search Committee, Black Rock University, Buffalo, NY 14200.

Comments on Preceding Advertisement

- Position description is most specific leading to suspicion that the successful candidate has been predetermined.
- Requests transcripts and recommendations with initial application. This will be a great deal of material for the college to handle if there are many applications. However, the applicant pool may be small with such a highly specific set of qualifications.
- Reasonable description of the college is provided.

BLACK ROCK UNIVERSITY

Early Childhood/Elementary Education: Black Rock University. Starting August 22, 19--. Teach Early Child & Elementary Education courses, supervise field experience in tri-college cooperative education program, coordinate Early Childhood Education program. Master's degree required. Doctorate preferred. Salary commensurate with qualifications & experience. Applications accepted until position is filled. Send credentials to Academic Dean, Black Rock University, Buffalo, NY 14200.

Comments on Preceding Advertisement
- Rank is not specified.
- There is no information about the college.
- There is no mention of tenure/non tenure.

SOCIOLOGY / SOCIAL WORK

Tenure track position at Assistant or Associate rank beginning September 1, 19--. Ph.D. in sociology with Quantitative Research Methods required. MSW and proficiency in Urban Sociology, Crime and Delinquency and Complex Organization highly desirable. Send letter of application, vita, transcripts and three letters of reference to Dr. Ian Smith, Black Rock University, Box 0002, Buffalo, NY 14200.

Comments on Preceding Advertisement
- There is no information about the university or the department.
- Salary range is not mentioned.
- Transcripts and letters of reference are requested with the initial application.

BLACK ROCK UNIVERSITY

Has openings for the following positions:

Counselor in the area of Student Services;
Counselor in the area of Special Services;
Instructor — Psychology/Sociology;
Instructor — Business Education and Automated Office Systems;
Instructor — Technical/Vocational Education.

Black Rock is an attractive suburb of Buffalo, New York with an excellent school system, numerous cultural agencies and all recreational advantages of being located on the Great Lakes. Canada is a few miles from the city.

Applications, resumes, confidential files and personal statements should be received by June 21, 19--. Submit to:

Personnel Office
Black Rock University
Buffalo, New York 14200

Comments on Preceding Advertisement

- Several disciplines are mentioned in one advertisement. It may not be read as carefully as an advertisement that was listed under a single discipline. However, in this case, the display advertisement was supplemented by ads in the classified columns under the particular discipline with the notation "See our display ad on page 55."
- Salary range is not mentioned.
- There is little information about the college itself.

MEDIA COMMUNICATIONS INSTRUCTORS — (2) full time for Media Communications Program. Positions become available January, 19--. To teach introductory and elective courses in theory, writing for media, journalism and reporting. Ph.D. preferred. Send resume and names addresses and telephone numbers of three referees to:

> Director of Personnel
> Jones Hall, Black Rock University
> Buffalo, NY 14200

Comments on Preceding Advertisement

- There is no information about the institution or the department.
- Salary and rank are not mentioned
- The ad states that a Ph.D. is preferred but does not indicate what is acceptable.

EMPLOYMENT COUNSELOR: Full time in Career, Counseling and Advisement Services. Responsibilities include but are not limited to the following: coordinating job development system for full and part time students; developing and maintaining contacts with employers through on-site visits, mailings, telephone calls, on campus recruitment program. Supervise part time job referral service, providing job hunting assistance for seniors and alumni, compile annual placement report. Baccalaureate degree required. Master's in Student Personnel preferred. Must have own transportation. Send resume to:

> Ms Mary Margaret O'Brien, Director,
> Counseling and Advisement Center
> Bison Hall, Black Rock University
> Buffalo, NY 14200

Comments on Preceding Advertisement

- There is no information about the university.
- There is no information about the student population—an important element in this ad.
- There is no closing date for applications.
- No salary information is contained in this ad.

BLACK ROCK UNIVERSITY

Black Rock University is located in an excellent suburb of Buffalo, New York, has a student population of 2,000 and offers baccalaureate degrees in Education, Human Services, Business, Art, Music, Media Communications and Liberal Studies. Masters' degrees are offered in Education and Allied Health Sciences. University personnel are highly visible in the affairs of the community.

HUMAN SERVICES—Full-time position to teach four courses, advise and assist with student recruiting, provide service to the university and the community. Ph.D. in an appropriate discipline required. A state license as a counselor is an asset.

CHILD AND YOUTH SERVICES—Two full-time positions. Teach twelve hours per week in courses that prepare students in the fields of child welfare, residential care centers, foster parent programs, domestic violence shelters and other youth oriented human service facilities. One position will be involved with the development of the master's degree in family counseling. Ph.D. in appropriate discipline or MSW with progress towards doctorate essential.

MEDIA COMMUNICATIONS—Full-time instructor for Media Communications. Strong theoretical and practical background. To be assigned courses in Media Communication Theory, Media Communications Law and Ethics, Writing for Media.

Salary and rank for all positions in relation to qualifications.

APPLICATIONS—Send a letter addressing the qualifications specified, a copy of the curriculum vita and a list of five referees with telephone numbers and addresses to Dr. William Orange, Assistant to the Provost, Black Rock University, Buffalo, NY 14200.

Comments on Preceding Advertisement

- A single advertisement for positions in three different fields may not attract as much attention as an advertisement for each position under the caption indicating the field.

```
┌─────────────────────────────────────────────────┐
│          VICE PRESIDENT FOR ACADEMIC AFFAIRS      │
│      Black Rock University is seeking a Vice President for Academic │
│   Affairs. The vice president is the chief academic officer and reports │
│   directly to the president. He/she is the acting president in the presi- │
│   dent's absence. The deans of the schools of Education, Business Ad- │
│   ministration, Humanities and Sciences report directly to the vice presi- │
│   dent. The university seeks an individual with a Ph.D. or equivalent, │
│   experience in post-secondary administration, successful teaching and │
│   scholarly activities and evidence of sensitivity to the many constituen- │
│   cies of the university. Applications and nominations will be received │
│   until April 15. Women and members of minority groups are encourag- │
│   ed to apply. │
│      Send inquiries, nominations and applications to: │
│                 Dr. FitzPatrick Jamieson, Chair │
│                 Vice President Search Committee │
│                 c/o Office of the President │
│                 Black Rock University │
│                 Buffalo, NY 14200 │
└─────────────────────────────────────────────────┘
```

Comments on Preceding Advertisement

- There is no information about the university.
- Salary is not mentioned.
- There is no information about the town or area in which the university is located.

Once advertisements have been formulated and placed in appropriate publications and distributed to various university departments and placement services, the search committee should prepare to receive and respond to applications.

LEGAL CONCERNS

Inaccurate Advertisements

Advertisements for the position should be concise and accurate. They should set forth, at a minimum the job description, qualifications expected, the name of the person to whom applications are to be sent, and the deadline for the receipt of applications.

Restricted Placing of Advertisements

Advertisements should be placed where they are likely to be seen by a wide variety of applicants, including minorities and women. This may require placement in a number of newspapers and journals, as well as mailing to institutions.

Chapter IV

Receiving and Responding to Applicants

At the outset it is necessary for the contact person to have a system ready for receiving and recording applications. If a word processor or computer is available, applications may be recorded there. A log should be maintained to record all incoming applications. The log should contain the title of the available position, the date the application was received, and several spaces to indicate the results of the initial screening. Applications may also be recorded in a simple hand written log on sheets of paper or 3x5 file cards (which allows the contact person to alphabetize the cards).

As applicants are eliminated, the information should be recorded. Records in the log (whether on word processor, computer, sheets of paper or file cards) should contain the following information:

```
Applicant Name _____  Position _____
Initial Application Received              ___(date)___
Application Acknowledged                  ___(date)___
File Complete and Given to Search Committee   ___(date)___
    Results:
        Initial Review  _____
        Second Review  _____
        Third Review  _____
Applicant notified of elimination from process ___(date)___
Applicant Interviewed ___(date)___
Resulting Action_____
```

Upon elimination from the search or employment of the applicant the above information should be sent to Personnel/Affirmative Action and retained there according to college policy.

PRE-EMPLOYMENT INQUIRIES

Lawful	Unlawful*
1. Name	Maiden Name Name of mother, other relatives Mr/Mrs/Miss/Ms
2. Address	List of previous addresses How long at specific address (*OK: how long lived "in this area"*)
3. Education • extent • schools attended • degrees/diplomas	Avoid inflated educational requirements Dates of attendance
4. Work experience • Specific skills • Former employers —Names, addresses, Dates, Position held, Reason for leaving • Research interests and Publications	Avoid inflated requirement of work experience (*OK: Licensure, if clearly required*)
5. References • Personal & Professional —Persons who can vouch for qualifications and character —Person who referred them to this job	Reference from member of clergy
6. Are U.S. citizen or have legal right to work in U.S.	National origin/birthplace Whether are citizen of another country Whether are naturalized U.S. Citizen Date acquired citizenship
7.	Age
8.	Religious affiliation Church attended (*OK: For job description to state required working days, hours, shifts*)
9.	Race/color Supply photo
10.	Sex Marital Status

*unless **directly** related to qualifications for this particular position

Lawful	Unlawful*
10. (continued)	Number and ages of children Child bearing/rearing queries
11.	Height/weight
12.	General physical condition/ Handicap Previous workers compensation claims Identify diseases suffered (OK: Job offer contingent on passing job-related physical exam) (OK: After hired, may ask if there is any physical condition or handicap limiting ability to do job, and what accommoda- tion might be made to enable person to do job)
13.	Foreign language ability
14.	Arrests
15.	Convictions
16.	Ever denied a fidelity bond (OK: If a job requirement)
17.	Personal finances • charge accounts • bank accounts • credit rating Past wage garnishments Personal bankruptcy Home ownership Car ownership (OK: where required for job, may ask if have use of a car and have valid driver's license)
18.	Have relatives or friends who work for institution
19.	Who to notify in case of emergency
20.	List of clubs, societies, lodges of which one is a member
21.	Political affiliation
22.	Union membership

*unless **directly** related to qualifications for this particular position

RESPONDING

Each applicant that the college/university accepts* must be answered, preferably within the week of receipt. The acknowledgement should NOT be in an obviously duplicated form. With the advent of memory typewriters and word processing machines, it is reasonable to expect that the potential employer will use a modern method which makes each letter appear to be individually composed. The difference in cost between a properly addressed letter which has the same appearance as the text of the letter is negligible. The gain in the regard with which the institution will be held by the applicant when he/she receives a courteous letter which appears to be individual, is incalculable.

The letter of acknowledgement is a simple note and states that the application has been received and will receive the attention of the search committee shortly.

Letter of Acknowledgement

Dear _____

    Your application for a faculty position in _____ has been received.[1] In order to evaluate your application we need to have the enclosed Special Data Form completed and in our hands by _____.[2]

    Please note that the Special Data Form asks you to indicate which courses you are best prepared to teach. Course descriptions are enclosed for your review.[3]

    I am also enclosing some materials about the Black Rock area and the university.

    We plan to conclude the search as soon as possible and keep you notified about our progress.[4]

Sincerely,

_____

Chair, Search Committee

Important Elements in Letter of Acknowledgement
(1) Application acknowledged.
(2) Form must be completed and on hand to complete application.

---

*Colleges are not required to accept all applications. Every search seems to bring a number of "circulars," i.e. duplicated letters with blank spaces where names and addresses are inserted by the applicant. These usually are not bona fide applications as they do not provide original letters addressed to the specific requirements of the position. Sometimes a resume with some message scrawled on it is received. In such instances, mass circulation letters may be rejected at the initial screening since they do not address the particular position.

(3) Applicant must indicate which courses he/she can teach.

(4) Applicant will be notified as to results.

Alternate Letter of Acknowledgement

Dear _____ :

Your application for the position of Associate Dean of Humanities has been received.[1] In order to evaluate your application fully, we ask you to complete the Special Data Form enclosed.

Please note that the Special Data Form asks questions about specific administrative experience. The Special Data Form must be in our hands by _____ .[2]

The University has an Affirmative Action Plan which requires that we request you to complete the enclosed Affirmative Action Form and return it directly to our Affirmative Action Office. A stamped envelope is enclosed for your convenience. Note that the form is to be returned directly to the Affirmative Action Office and will not be given to the Search Committee.[3]

The search will probably continue over several months, but we will notify you as to what actions are taken at the earliest possible point in the search.[4]

Sincerely;

_____

Chair, Search Committee

Important Elements in Letter of Acknowledgement

(1) Application acknowledged.

(2) Special Data Form must be completed and returned by a specific date.

(3) Affirmative Action Form not to be given to search committee.

(4) Applicant will be informed about search results when a decision has been made about him/her.

A letter of acknowledgement may also contain information about the institution, the community, the particular position and any other insights which the committee wishes the applicant to have in order to know more about the setting. If the additional materials are overly heavy, they may be sent by a different class of mail in a separate envelope.

Affirmative Action Form

Dear Applicant:

    Black Rock University is required to maintain records, for affirmative action purposes, on applicants for all positions. We request that you complete the following information and mail it directly to the Affirmative Action Office as indicated. The information contained on this form will <u>not</u> be given to the search committee, nor will it have any effect on your application.

    The completion of this form is voluntary on the part of the applicant.

Name (Optional) _____

Position for which applied _____

Sex: Male _____; Female _____   Age _____

Ethnicity: Black   _____   Asian   _____
          Pacific Islander   _____   Hispanic _____
          Caucasian (not of   American
          Hispanic origin) _____   Indian   _____

Handicapped? yes _____; no _____

If yes, what accommodations required _____

Are you a veteran of the Viet Nam era? yes _____; no _____

SPECIAL DATA FORM

    It often is wise to include a special application form which addresses the qualifications for the particular position. It may even be helpful to include course outlines, if the position is a teaching position. Applicants may be asked to express their abilities to teach each course. For certain administrative positions applicants are often asked to write out statements of philosophy or respond to open ended questions.*

    If personal statements or Special Data Forms are enclosed, there should be a notification in the letter of acknowledgement indicating when the replies are due in the hands of the search committee.

    For each application received, the search committee should have a checklist to note which items required for completion of the application have been received and whether or not they were received by the closing date(s).

---

*If open ended questions are used, the search committee should know what answers it wishes to find. A list of the important points sought should be part of the list of criteria developed by the search committee.

BLACK ROCK UNIVERSITY
Buffalo, NY 14200

SPECIAL DATA FORM
Computer Informations Systems Program

Complete all items. Do not write "see resume."[1]

I. Name _____

   Address _____
   _____
   _____

   Telephones: Home (____)_____ Office (____)_____
   Other telephone where you may be contacted (____)_____
   What days and hours are best to call you?
      home _____ office _____ other _____[2]
   If you are selected for an interview, when are you available?
   _____

II. Citizenship
   U.S. citizen?   yes _____   no_____
   If not a U.S. citizen, do you have a legal right to work in U.S.?
      yes _____   no_____
      please explain _____[3]

III. How do you meet the requirements of the position as advertised?
   _____[4]
   _____
   _____
   _____
   _____

IV. Education (list most recent study first)
   Degree   Institution
   _____   _____
   _____   _____
   _____   _____

V. Current or Last Position
   a. From   To   Position/Title   Duties
   _____   _____   _____   _____
   Employer   _____   _____
   Why left   _____   _____

   Previous Positions
   b. From   To   Position/Title   Duties
   _____   _____   _____   _____
   Employer   _____   _____
   Why left   _____   _____
   c. From   To   Position/Title   Duties
   _____   _____   _____   _____
   Employer   _____   _____
   Why left   _____   _____

45

VI. Courses for which prepared:
From the enclosed list of courses, please list courses which you can
teach and at what level of confidence for you.

Course	Confident	Fairly Confident	Need More Preparation	Course	Confident	Fairly Confident	Need More Preparation

VII. List Publications

VIII. List persons who are able to evaluate your qualifications for the
position.

Name	Address	Phone Nos.	Relation to You
		home _____	
		office _____	
		home _____	
		office _____	
		home _____	
		office _____	

Comments on Special Data Form

Overall, this is a relatively short form designed to get sufficient preliminary information from applicants in specific terms.

(1) The search committee wants this information in this particular form so that it doesn't have to search through many vitae, each in a different form, to cull out the needed information

(2) Getting the numerous telephone numbers and the days and hours at which applicants can be reached will save callers much frustration when trying to contact applicants.

(3) Over the past fifteen years, the United States has received a new type immigrant. Millions of persons from Asia, Latin America and Africa have arrived, many of them to take advanced work at American universities. This means that many applications for positions will come from persons who are not native English speakers. They also may be on student visas which do not allow them to undertake full-time positions.

Before inviting a non-native English speaker for an interview, it is best to speak to that person on the telephone to determine if his/her English speaking ability is adequate for the requirements of the position.

In the case where the best candidate for a position is a person on a student visa, it is essential to contact the college attorney before offering him/her a contract.

(4) The applicant has an opportunity to state how he/she fits the requirement of the position.

(5) Only the last three employers' names are requested. If there is a reason to have more employment history, additional space may be added.

(6) Applicants are given a list of courses or duties that they may be asked to perform. This area of the application asks exactly what their competencies are.

Follow-up to Acknowledgement of Application

This letter (see next page) may be desirable when applicant is interesting to the search committee but all information is not on hand. This letter may also be used to encourage a more rapid response when applicants for a crucial position are few in number.

Important Elements in Letter (next page)

(1) Employer still interested but wants more information.

(2) Materials must be sent by specified date if application is to be considered.

Dear _____ :

    We refer to your application for the position of _____.
To date the following information has not been received:

    a. Letter of application addressing qualifications for the position;

    b. Completed Special Data form for the position;

    c. Statement of personal philosophy;

    d. Names, addresses, telephone numbers of persons who can provide recommendations for you;

    e. University placement file.[1]

    When the above information is received your application will be ready for initial screening. The screening will commence on ____(date)____. If your file is complete by that time, I shall forward it to the Search Committee.[2]

Sincerely,

_____
Personnel Officer

INITIAL SCREENING

Once the closing date has arrived, all materials requested from candidates should be on hand. If applicants have not sent in all materials, these applications may be eliminated. However, some institutions are anxious to have the largest number of completed applications possible for consideration, so a reminder letter may be used several weeks before the closing date.

The initial screening is simply a device for eliminating those applicants who have not provided the requested information needed by the search committee to review the application properly. If all requested materials have been received and the candidate has the qualifications necessary for the position, the applicant has passed the initial screening. However, if all requested materials are not on hand, the applicant has not passed the initial screening. Similarly, if the applicant does not have the minimal education or experiential qualifications, he/she has not passed the initial screening. Applicants who fail to pass the initial screening should be notified as soon as possible, and their files set aside. Once the first "cut" has been made, a more thorough review of the applications takes place.

```
┌─────────────────────────────────────────────────────────────┐
│                    INITIAL SCREENING                         │
│                                                              │
│  Name  _____          │
│                                                              │
│  Has applicant sent all requested materials by due date?    │
│      Cover letter addressing qualifications      _____     │
│      Resume related to position                  _____     │
│      List of referees                            _____     │
│      Completed Special Data Form                 _____     │
│      Other Information                           _____     │
│                                                              │
│  Does Applicant meet qualifications required?               │
│      Degree(s)                                   _____     │
│      Experience:                                            │
│          Administration/Staff                    _____     │
│          Teaching                                _____     │
│          Scholary research and publications     _____     │
│      Other _____                  _____     │
│                                                              │
│            _____                             │
└─────────────────────────────────────────────────────────────┘
```

The purpose of the Initial Screening is simply to determine if the applicant has the requirements listed in the advertisement. It is a quantitative not qualitative review.

THE SECOND REVIEW

The second review is more qualitative in character than is the initial screening. During the second review the search committee examines the material sent by applicants with great care and assesses the degree to which the applicant has met or exceeded the criteria established by the committee. At this point, it might be necessary for the search committee to contact applicants to ask more specifically about the way in which the applicant feels that he/she meets the established criteria. For example, a search committee charged with finding a researcher may wish to know more about the type of research the applicant has done and the persons with whom he/she has worked. The search committee may wish to know how these colleagues perceived the applicant's work. The search committee also may wish to explore the applicant's continued interest in the position. The major purpose of any telephone conversation with the applicant is to explore how he/she meets the criteria. It is also wise to record any statements as to the abilities and qualifications claimed by the applicant so that referees may be asked to comment on these specifics. (Naturally, if a recording device is to be used during the call, the permission of the applicant must be secured before proceeding.) The ap-

SECOND REVIEW SCORING FORM
Black Rock University

Candidate: _____

Position: _____Dean, School of Arts and Science_____

CRITERIA		HOW DOES CANDIDATE MEET CRITERIA?	SCORE 1 = Min. 5 = Ideal
Ideal	Acceptable*		
Education Doctorate in a field taught by School	Masters in a field taught in School and a doctorate in Higher Education		
Experience 1. 10 years teaching in higher education	1. 5 years teaching in higher education		
2. Senior level administration at a research oriented university	2. Minimum of 3 years as department head or similar position in research oriented university		
Personal/ Professional 1. Leads in maintaining shared governance	1. Accepts existing faculty governance structure		
2. Superior negotiating skills	2. Can act as part of negotiating team		
3. Nationally known in field. Publications	3. Well acquainted with a number of leaders in field. Publications.		
4. Highly successful grant writer	4. Aware of grant opportunities		
5. Superior skills in communication	5. Above average in communication skills		

NOTE: Scoring can be adjusted to reflect the value each characteristic has to the Search Committee

* - Minimum as advertised

50

SECOND REVIEW SCORING FORM
Black Rock University

Candidate:_____ Position: Assist./Assoc. Prof., Business Admin._____

CRITERIA		HOW DOES CANDIDATE MEET CRITERIA?	SCORE 1=Min. 5=Ideal
Ideal	Acceptable*		
Education D.B.A.	M.B.A. + C.P.A. or M.B.A. + significant work toward doctorate		
Experience 1. 5 years working in a business field as a major administrator	1. 2 years in business in mid-management		
2. 2 years full-time equivalent in post-secondary institution(s)	2. Some teaching exience, at least as a teaching assistant		
Personal/Professional 1. High energy level	1. Willing to put in reasonable amount of time on departmental projects		
2. Initiative	2. If not leader, then a strong competent follower		
3. Highly personable	3. Nonabrasive		
4. Depth of understanding of Black Rock students	4. Willingness to learn of needs and characteristics of student population		
5. Extensive list of referred publications	5. Shows potential as a writer/researcher		
6. Holds or held leadership positions in professional organizations	6. Is aware of current trends and issues in the profession		
7. Proven record as a community leader	7. Interest in community affairs and willingness to be active		

NOTE: Scoring can be adjusted to reflect the value each
      characteristic has to the Search Committee

* - Minimum as advertised

plicant should also be told that his referees are to be contacted and that his/her transcripts should be sent as soon as possible.

By the end of the second review applicants become serious candidates. The list of applicants should be severely reduced. Ideally, there will be ten to fifteen candidates on the semi-final list. They are persons about whom the committee feels fairly confident but who must be investigated further.

To Unsuccessful Applicants After Initial or Second Review

Dear _____:
    The Search Committee for the position of _____ met on October 14, to review applications. After considerable deliberation[1] the Committee decided that other applicants meet the requirements for the position more closely.[2] Therefore, you are no longer under active consideration.[3]
    The Committee asked me to express its appreciation for the time you took to apply for the position.[4]
Sincerely,

_____
Personnel Officer

Important Elements in Letter Above

(1) The application was fully considered.
(2) Other applications were more suited for further consideration.
(3) Applicant is no longer being considered.
(4) Applicant is thanked for his/her time.

To Applicants Still Being Considered after the Second Review

Dear _____:
    The Search Committee wishes me to inform you that after several reviews you are still under consideration for the position of _____.[1]
    At this time it is important that we have copies of your transcripts sent from your college or university directly to us.[2] We are also writing to those persons whom you listed as referees.[3]
    If there is any other information you wish to present to the Committee, please do so by ____(date)____.
Sincerely,

_____
Personnel Officer

Important Elements in Preceding Letter
(1) The candidate is still under consideration.
(2) Transcripts must be sent from university.
(3) Referees will be contacted.
(4) The committee is close to making a recommendation. If the candidate is truly interested, it is now worth the time and money to make the best possible presentation.

RECOMMENDATIONS FROM REFEREES

The search committee now requests recommendations from the persons named as referees in the original application letter. Any other persons whose names come up in the telephone conversation with the applicant may also be contacted. The letters to referees should be specific. The duties and qualifications of the position should be outlined, and the referee asked to address his/her remarks to the qualifications. It is also important that the relationship of the referee to the candidate be described.

To Referees

Dear _____:

Dr. John Jones is a finalist in our search to fill the position of _____ at this college.[1] He has given us your name as one who can comment on his qualifications and experience.

A description of the position is enclosed. We would appreciate a letter from you that addresses Dr. Jones' qualifications and ability to perform the duties outlined in the position description.[2] It will also be helpful if you can indicate in what capacity you have known Dr. Jones.[3] The Search Committee will be reviewing recommendations on ___(date)___ so your early reply will be helpful.

Sincerely,

_____
Personnel Officer

Important Elements in Letter Above
(1) Search Committee is seriously interested in candidate so referee can see that recommendation is important.
(2) Referee is asked to address specific qualifications of candidate to perform duties.
(3) The relationship of the referee to the candidate may indicate to some extent the weight that should be given to the recommendation.
(4) The referee is given a date by which the recommendation is needed.

References should be examined carefully. There should be two parts to the recommendation: the qualifications of the candidate for the position should be addressed and, hopefully, there will be some indication as to how the candidate acts in interpersonal relationships.

A candidate should not be eliminated because of one poor reference. However, if a particular negative characteristic appears in several letters, it should be investigated by telephone with the referees.

It is most important to read the letters carefully as it is sometimes the case that a referee will write what appears at first to be a glowing recommendation. After reviewing the letter several times, however, it may become apparent that the former or current duties of the candidate were described but there was no qualitative assessment of how those duties were performed.

There also are letters which may have phrases like "While she does not suffer fools, gladly, she . . ." What does the writer mean? Does he mean that the candidate is arrogant, that she has poor interpersonal skills or is very demanding? Also, what is the assessment of the search committee as to how important this factor is when weighed against the needs of the institution?

In cases where the phraseology of the writer causes the search committee to be concerned about personal or professional qualifications, it may be best for a conference call to be made to the referee. Direct questions should be asked about any aspects of the letter which seem to convey a covert warning. More often than not, a telephone call will elicit a more direct response to areas of concern than will a written response.

In addition to those persons listed as referees by the candidate, it is often wise to contact other persons who have been closely associated with the candidate in his/her recent or current position. This may mean telephoning a chairperson, dean, or even a president. Of course, the candidate should be aware that such a call might be made.

Referees should be called to ascertain how competent the candidate is in his/her academic or administrative field. Questions about the effectiveness of the candidate's dealings with peers, superiors, students, and others are also quite appropriate.

In all cases, it is important to check the candidate's perception of what he has accomplished with the perceptions of the referee on the same subject.

Preparation for Calling Referees

Prior to telephoning a referee, it might be wise to telephone the candidate. Conference calls with all or most of the search committee present are not unusual. Sometimes a committee will ask the candidate how he would describe him/herself. It is also informative to ask the candidate how the persons whom he/she has listed as referees will describe him/her. "What might Mr. Brown say about your behavior in crises?" "What will Dr. Rodney say about your competence in fund raising?"

These questions make the candidate aware that you will follow-up on a reference check. They also make him/her aware of the kind of talents being sought. The conversation with the candidate may also help raise the right questions to be asked of referees.

Cautions

Do not ask candidates questions about religious preference (unless it relates directly to the position and is listed as part of the criteria). Don't ask female candidates about how they might find child care, or whether their spouses wil approve of what they are doing. Avoid any condescending remarks about persons of particular racial or religious groups, and be unusually careful not to indicate an institutional preference for employing males, females, blacks, whites, persons over or under a certain age or with handicaps. A discussion of political preferences is also onerous.

CHECKLIST FOR RECOMMENDATIONS FROM REFEREES

	Yes	No
1. Does the referee state relationship to the candidate?	____	____
2. Is specific knowledge of the candidate's subject matter background mentioned?	____	____
3. Is the matter of quality of research and publications mentioned?	____	____
4. Are candidate's duties in current position noted?	____	____
5. Does referee state how well candidate performs his/her duties?	____	____
6. Are interpersonal relationship abilities noted?	____	____
7. Are administrative skills mentioned?	____	____
8. Is there a reference to entry level of the candidate?	____	____
9. Is the question of the candidate's initiative mentioned?	____	____
10. Are specific instances of excellent performance documented?	____	____
11. Does any part of the letter raise additional questions about the candidate's skills, abilities, knowledge or judgment?	____	____

12. Are there negative comments that are echoed in other letters of reference? ____ ____
13. Are there positive remarks similar to those written by other referees for this candidate? ____ ____
14. Do there seem to be any hidden messages (covert warnings)? ____ ____
15. Are any personality traits described? ____ ____
16. Are student-professor or superior-subordinate relations mentioned? ____ ____

THIRD REVIEW

Once all recommendations and investigations have been completed, the search committee should meet to list candidates in the order in which they meet criteria. Each committee member should complete an evaluation form and give it to the chairperson. Top listed candidates will be invited to an interview.

INTERVIEW POLICY

There are several different policies for interviewing. Some institutions will interview only one candidate. If that person satisfies the search committee, he/she will be recommended for the position to the appropriate administrator. If a candidate is not satisfactory to the committee, a second candidate will be interviewed and so on.

Most colleges tend to interview three to five top candidates and recommend the one whom the search committee prefers.

Some colleges may interview as many as ten or twelve candidates before making a selection. This is more common when seeking to fill a major position.

There are also colleges that will hold a series of interviews. There wil be an initial interview for ten or twelve persons. Then there will be a second round with perhaps three to five of the first group being asked to return. Some colleges have been known to have a third round when the two surviving candidates are reviewed.

The contact person must know what policy is to be followed before arranging interviews.

LEGAL CONCERNS

Inequitable Review of Applications

It is essential that all applicants know that all applications will be accorded equitable consideration and review. The law requires, and applicants have the right to expect, that applications will be judged against the stated measures, namely the position description and position qualifications. The procedure followed by a search committee and its staff should be designed to assure not only that all applicants in fact are treated equitably, but also that they perceive that they have been so treated.

Poor Procedure for Receipt and Response to Applications

Persons designated to receive and respond to applications should be clear about what procedure is to be followed and what they are authorized to say.

When applications are received, they should be kept in a safe place in the care of a responsible person. It is a good idea to send an acknowledgement to the applicant, not only as a courtesy but to confirm that the applicant's file has been opened for due consideration along with those of all other applicants.

Lack of Confidentiality of References

Persons to be contacted for references for applicants should be informed whether or not their letters will be kept confidential and not revealed to the applicant or others.

Open Meeting Laws

A number of states have statutes that provide for public access to certain information and meetings where public decision-making takes place. If yours is a public institution, review in advance with legal counsel whether your state has open meeting or sunshine laws and, if so, how they affect searches for personnel at your institution.

Chapter V

Interviewing

IMPORTANCE OF PERSONAL INTERVIEWS

The interviewing of candidates is the climax of a long arduous process. It is the event for which months of preparation have been made. It is imperative that every effort be made to see that it is a smooth and successful experience. Interviewing and the immediate follow-up give the search committee the opportunity to see its work come to fruition. However, it also may be a time of great disappointment. A candidate may not seem nearly as attractive when present on campus or an institution may not seem attractive to the candidate. Then too, a person with the authority to veto a candidate may decide to do so.*

Interviewing is important for a number of reasons:

1. The search committee can assess the candidate's communication abilities, appearance, personality traits, thinking habits and motivation.
2. The interviewee may reveal the extent of his/her true interest in the position. (The amount of background material about the college that the candidate has unearthed may be one indicator of real interest.)
3. In conversation, the candidate often will reveal information about him/herself that might not be obtained elsewhere. Most people are willing to say more about themselves than they will write down.
4. Any lingering questions about a candidate's academic, research, or administrative abilities and interests may be clarified.
5. The candidate's reactions or attitudes towards real issues or problems on campus may be explored at length.

---

*It is conceivable that a dean may veto the appointment of a potential faculty member, that a vice president may veto a search committee choice for a position, or that any number of administrators may do the same thing. These possibilities make it vital that persons who have veto power over the appointment of candidates be consulted about the suitability of candidates *before* they are invited to the campus.

PREPARING FOR THE INTERVIEW

During the interviewing process all interested parties with legitimate concerns should get the opportunity to meet the candidate and learn about him or her. Meetings with potential peers, subordinates and/or superiors are important for the candidate as well as for the institution for it is quite possible that the candidate may not wish to pursue his/her candidacy if some of the human factors do not auger well.

All of the parties who meet with the candidate should make their opinions about the candidate known to the search committee.

Once the search committee has decided on a short list, the supervisor involved should be notified. The probable costs of travel and accommodation should be a matter of mutual agreement and the necessary funds should be made available.

A decision should be made as to whether the search committee should schedule one meeting at a time, recommending the first person whom they feel meets the criteria, or whether a number of candidates should be interviewed and the most attractive from the group of interviewees recommended. For a faculty position, three to five persons are usually interviewed and listed in descending order of acceptability to the search committee.

For major administrative positions, ten or more persons may be interviewed as the committee may be asked to give the prospective supervisor of the selectee three names for consideration.

In preparing for the interviews the contact person must see that the following is done:

1. **Set up informal and formal meetings** arranging firm meeting times. Informal meetings are with interested parties who can have more relaxed conversations exploring how the candidate will interact with various constituencies of the college

    Formal meetings are those meetings with the search committee and persons to whom the successful candidate will report.

    Informal meetings might include prospective faculty members meeting with the staff of the Dean of Student Affairs, faculty members from other disciplines, or even local community people.

2. **Arrange travel and accommodation plans** with the candidate. Some colleges have travel agents with whom they prefer to make travel arrangements. They may also have hotels or motels where they prefer that their guests stay. Colleges may even have guest rooms on campus for candidates.

3. **Discuss travel reimbursement with the candidate.** Each institution has its own unique method of reimbursement. For candidates for faculty or minor administrative positions some institutions do not offer reimbursement; others may offer a flat sum to cover a part of the expenses while others cover all reasonable costs for the in-

terview. There are also some colleges which will pay only a fixed percentage of the travel and accommodation costs.

Some colleges have a policy that they will pay all reasonable expenses but if the candidate is offered a position and rejects it, he/she will not be reimbursed.

Normally, candidates for major positions have all reasonable expenses paid and may expect to be entertained by the search committee. However, even for major positions there are a few colleges that do not pay any expenses for interviews.

When the candidate will be paid is pertinent. Some institutions ask the candidate to pay all of his/her expenses in advance and claim reimbursement for them after the interview. Other colleges will arrange air tickets and hotels and have the accounts sent directly to the college. Incidental expenses are claimed after the interview.

After the telephone call discussing travel reimbursement all policies regarding expenses and reimbursement should be confirmed in writing and sent by certified mail to the candidate.

4. **Prepare an itinerary for the candidate.** All persons to be met by the candidate should know where, when and why. The candidate should be given a copy of the interview schedule.

5. **Arrange for the candidate's spouse to be occupied.** Candidates may bring spouses to investigate a location not familiar to them. In such cases, the usual courtesy is to give the spouse a tour of the town and provide information on schools, work possibilities, housing or whatever other topics are important.

FUNCTION OF THE INTERVIEWS

The interview should be conducted in a manner that allows college personnel to get to know candidates reasonably well. The candidate also should have an opportunity to gain an understanding of the institution, its problems, major issues and expectations. To ensure that the interview achieves its purposes, there should be an interview plan.

Recently, one east coast college system was discussed by a number of former applicants for major positions. Candidates for academic and student personnel deanships discovered that they had all been treated in the same curt manner. Each candidate was informed that he/she would receive only a partial reimbursement for interview expenses. As the expenses were modest, the candidates each agreed to attend the interviews.

When a candidate arrived on a campus, he/she was met by a faculty host who provided a brief campus tour, took the candidate to lunch in the campus cafeteria and then delivered the candidate to the search committee where a one hour interview was conducted by ten to twelve people. (The mix of the search committee changed during the interview as members entered and left to perform other duties.) At the end of the interview, each candidate was thanked and he/she went home.

In each case the candidate discovered that ten persons were interviewed for the position and that there were one or two "in-house" candidates. In each case an in-house candidate was chosen for the position. Before the formal interview, the candidate heard only one person's views about the institution and in several cases the host who provided the campus tour and lunch was a disgruntled or alienated professor who did not portray the campus political situation in a good light.

The ex-candidates, all successfully settled in other positions, agreed that they had been handled in a careless manner that made them question the genuineness of the process of this college system. (They all suspected that the search was pro forma and the "winning" candidate had been selected by the administration well in advance of the interviews.)

The colleges' candidates made unnecessary expenditures of time and money, neither party got to know about the other, and the reputation of these colleges suffered in respect to treatment of candidates. The colleges did not take time to estimate how the candidates would fit the environment, relate to other human beings, or perform as leaders. While the candidates did see some of the physical plant of the colleges, they had little opportunity to learn about the human dimensions of the institution. Much more is needed if the interviewing process is to be mutually beneficial.

The whole atmosphere surrounding the interviewing process needs to be one that encourages candidates and hosts alike to explore the competencies of the other. The process needs to be organized, friendly, yet businesslike.

Issues and Problems

Over and above the materials sent to the candidates, there is a need to inform them about issues and problems that exist. Often there are major academic and policy issues on the minds of faculty members and administrators about which the candidates should know. If there is a curricular revision in process, the candidate for a faculty position should be aware of it so that he/she may address related issues if they arise at interviews. Similarly, candidates for administrative positions should be aware of important issues that would affect their behaviors if selected for the positions. Any issues with which successful candidates must deal should be brought to the candidate's attention before he/she is asked for an opinion during an interview. This is often done over the telephone when arranging the interview.

The line between accurate information and gossipy partisanship can be fuzzy at times so it is important that the contact person be most careful but frank in explaining any situations which may affect the candidate's willingness to accept a position if offered. It is also true that some candidates have withdrawn from consideration when certain issues are called to their attention. And this may be fair for all concerned as it saves unnecessary expenditures of time and money where a candidate does not wish to confront certain problems or issues. Again, this should be discussed *before* candidates are brought for formal interviews. The major purpose of calling the candidate's attention to campus issues is to enable him/her to prepare to answer questions that may be raised during interviews. It also enables him/her to formulate questions of importance to him/herself.

INFORMAL INTERVIEWS

Arrangements are often made for a candidate to meet a broad section of the college community in relaxed surroundings. It is common for one or several persons to meet a candidate at the airport, take him or her to the hotel and have a meal together. At these informal meetings the candidate and host(s) tend to have unstructured conversations. The host(s) might talk discreetly about families, schools in the area, social and cultural life. The candidate may want to know about work opportunities for his/her spouse. The host(s) at these informal meetings should come prepared with "small talk" topics. The topics should be chosen so that the candidate reveals something about him/herself. Hobbies, activities, interests, travel are all good topics for light conversation. However, there should be no attempt to pry into matters that deal with areas that are not related to the candidate's suitability for the position, particularly where a candidate might perceive prejudice.

The hosts should be persons who have a good grasp of the non-academic needs of the institution. Is there a need for a social organizer or joiner? Do student clubs need advisors? Is there a desire to increase participation in cultural activities? How well might the candidate contribute to the non-instructional life of the college?

In certain institutions or for particular positions these considerations may be totally irrelevant. Nevertheless, in close-knit institutions many personal factors may be important. Most institutions have no reason to ask questions about race, sex, age, handicaps, national origin or religion. However, as has been mentioned, some colleges may have requirements about personal behavior or religious convictions. These should have been addressed long before a candidate arrives on campus.

It is the function of informal meetings to make the candidate aware of the distinctive characteristics of the institution and the community and to make some observations as to how the candidate will "fit." This should be done in a balanced and realistic manner.

Many search committees miss opportunities for informal interviews. Some committees send a work-study student or maintenance person to pick up a candidate at an airport, thus losing the opportunity

INFORMAL MEETING OBSERVATIONS

Candidate _____ Date _____

Comments by _____

1. Was the candidate appropriately dressed for
   the occasion?   Yes_____ No_____
   Comment: _____

2. Did the candidate speak clearly and to the
   point?   Yes_____ No_____
   Comment: _____

3. Did it appear that the candidate had sought
   information about the College before
   arriving on campus?   Yes_____ No_____
   Comment: _____

4. Does the candidate seem genuinely inter-
   ested in the position?   Yes_____ No_____
   Comment: _____

5. Did the candidate make any remarks or
   comments that indicate that further informa-
   tion about him/her may be needed?   Yes_____ No_____
   Comment: _____

6. Did conversation with the candidate indicate that
   he/she has additional qualifications or qualities about which we have been unaware?   Yes_____ No_____
   Comment: _____

7. Did the candidate respond to any campus
   issues or concerns?   Yes_____ No_____
   Comment: _____

8. Does the candidate have non-academic
   interests that could be of benefit to the
   college community?   Yes_____ No_____
   Comment: _____

9. Did the candidate answer unanticipated ques-
   tions or comments well and effectively?   Yes_____ No_____
   Comment: _____

10. Other observations: _____
    _____
    _____
    _____
    _____

NOTE: The assessment is from persons who are not members of the
      search committee but who may have to interact on several
      levels with other members of the community. Therefore, the
      comments are an important part of the observations.

for an additional prospective colleague to meet the candidate. (Nevertheless, opinions of students and non-professionals may be valuable to some institutions.)

Search committees do not have to have formal evaluations from the hosts at informal meetings. However, some comments on the reactions to the candidate should be obtained.

SEMI-FORMAL INTERVIEW

A meeting between candidates for academic leadership positions and the faculty and student groups is common. Often a time is set for each group to assemble and have a question and answer session with a candidate. Attendance by faculty members or students usually depends on the number of candidates to be seen, the perception by the groups as to how important the position is and the hour and date for which the meeting is set (not too many people attend during final exams week).

Persons attending these meetings are asked to complete evaluation forms and return these to the chairperson of the search committee. The weight the committee gives to these evaluations need not be great unless the attendance at the semi-formal meetings was good for all the candidates. In many searches no one student or faculty member will have seen all the candidates. Unless there are unusually consistent evaluations on a candidate a fair comparison cannot be made. However, if a candidate who is particularly favored, by the search committee and other groups, receives highly favorable remarks that information should be weighed. This type of interview has an advantage. It is usually not possible to structure this meeting to a great extent. Questions and comments may be unexpected, irrelevant, hostile, sympathetic, self-serving or designed to embarrass a candidate. How a candidate handles the unanticipated at a meeting may be important to the search committee. Therefore, several members of the committee may wish to attend the semi-formal meetings and later provide the full committee with their perceptions about what occurred.

COLLOQUIUM OR DEMONSTRATION CLASS SESSION

It is common for prospective faculty members to conduct a colloquium or teach a demonstration lesson to a class. The colloquium would be attended by all interested parties and the class session would be observed by members of the search committee and evaluated by students and members of the committee. It can be argued that a colloquium or class session given under such circumstances is highly artificial. However, even under these circumstances, it is possible for an instructor to be at his/her best. Observers have a chance to see how well the prospective instructor handles organization of material, interacts with students, uses instructional materials, uses voice, eye contact techniques and uses any non-traditional teaching strategies.

EVALUATION OF COLLOQUIUM OR DEMONSTRATION CLASS SESSION

Name _____Date _____
Position _____
NOTE: The purpose of this colloquium or class session is to determine how well the candidate can express him/herself, interact with colleagues and students, use aids and materials, and demonstrate mastery of the subject matter.

		yes	no
1.	Was the candidate well-prepared?	___	___
2.	Did the candidate speak clearly and in a comprehensible manner?	___	___
3.	Was the presentation free from distracting mannerisms or gestures on the part of the candidate	___	___
4.	Were instructional aids well used?	___	___
5.	Did the candidate handle colleague and/or student questions or comments well?	___	___
6.	Was the purpose of the presentation clear	___	___
7.	Did the candidate appear to be comfortable with the subject matter?	___	___
8.	Did the candidate hold the attention of colleagues and students?	___	___
9.	Was the student-faculty interaction of high quality?	___	___
10.	Does the candidate seem to understand our students?	___	___

Comments: _____
_____
_____

The colloquium or class session should be arranged well in advance of the on-campus visit. Preferably, a regularly scheduled class will be used for the demonstration class session. The instructor in charge should give the candidate a list of topics he/she would like handled. The candidate should choose the topic he/she will teach and inform the regular instructor. The candidate should also request any special equipment or materials needed for the demonstration. Observers of the demonstration class session should make a formal but simple evaluation of it and the report should be sent to the search committee chairperson in time to use it for the overall evaluation. An individual member of the search committee should be responsible for getting the evaluations to the chairperson.

PREPARING THE FORMAL INTERVIEWING

Formal interviews are those conducted by search committees and persons who will be the individuals to whom the successful candidate reports. Formal interviews are major events in the search. They require a reasonable amount of planning to see that the outcome of the search is a success. The focus of the interviews can be narrowed with adequate preparation. The search committee already has verified the qualifications of candidates and has assurances from the candidate and others about competence, skills, knowledge and some personality traits. Some search committees even have a salary history from candidates.

THE FORMAL INTERVIEW

Committee Member Roles

The setting for a formal interview for a position in the academic world differs somewhat from that of the business world. In business the interviewer generally is a potential supervisor or a human resource development specialist. In the academic workplace the interviewers may be potential colleagues, peers, subordinates, supervisors, and/or students. The composition of the interviewing committees may create some concerns for interviewer and interviewee. Some possible pitfalls may be:

1. An interviewer who may be participating in the selection of a supervisor may be tempted to phrase questions to please the potential supervisor.
2. Sometimes members of a search committee will question a candidate about the performance of duties the questioner has never performed and therefore, the questioner will have difficulty evaluating the answer.
3. Interviewers may also ask questions which the candidate may be reluctant to answer for fear of placing him/herself at a future disadvantage. For example, a potential academic administrator may be asked how he would discipline a faculty member if necessary. The candidate might not like to have his/her strategies known in advance.
4. Interviewers may be tempted to ask questions that seem to make demands for promises of future behavior on the part of the successful candidate. while the question may be fair, a careful candidate might be justifiably reluctant to answer it.

To avoid problems that could be posed by such situations, the search committee should decide which questions *must* be asked. If a potential subordinate has an important question that he/she is uncomfortable about asking, then a member of the committee who is a possible peer or superior might ask it. Some colleges too, may be able to ask questions that are not appropriate for industry. A college with an orientation to a particular religious tradition might ask questions about religious beliefs and practices. Some colleges even require an affirmation of faith and will not employ users of alcohol or tobacco.

Publicly supported institutions may not ask questions related to religion, race, color, sex, age, national origin or handicap without risk. However, institutions with special missions do ask questions related to those missions. A historically black college may ask for evidence of concerns for the education of persons from minority groups; a community college usually asks about commitment to the "community college philosophy" and women's colleges have been known to ask about the special mission of preparing women for leadership roles in modern society.

It is important to emphasize the importance of fair and ethical interviewing. Searches have been terminated because of errors made by interviewers. Once a search has been contaminated by poor interviewing it usually is necessary to start all over. Thousands of hours and dollars will have been wasted if a search must be terminated or re-opened.

It is most important that the search committee prepare a method for asking questions. In some interviews each candidate is asked the same questions and the answers are compared. Critics of this method complain that this is little more than having candidates fill out questionnaires. Also, as each candidate is an individual, the uniqueness of a particular person may not show through use of such a questioning technique.

Some interviewers recommend that an outline of the areas to be covered be developed by the search committee and that questions be directed towards these areas. When a candidate's answer is particularly interesting, the matter may be pursued at greater depth. The areas to be explored and the questions to be developed must relate to the criteria for the position. There should be some agreement among the search committee members as to who will ask about certain areas. Some committee members may not have enough experience to ask insightful questions. For example, a faculty member on the search committee probably should not ask detailed questions about budget management of a candidate for an administrative position. Such questions might best be asked by someone familiar with the budget process.

Search committee members should also be prepared to have candidates decline to answer some questions. For example, candidates for deanships might be reluctant to reveal to faculty members of the search committee how he/she would deal with matters requiring curricular changes or deletions. He/she may not wish to divulge all the strategies used to accomplish his/her goals, and there may be other areas in administration where the candidate feels that he/she must reserve answers for fellow administrators or for self alone.

It is most unwise for a search committee to go to an interview unprepared. The kinds of questions to be asked must be developed: the chief questions in a line of questioning should be identified and the committee members must be reminded as to what kinds of questions are improper. The method for evaluating the formal interview should also be developed. Some instrument that measures the candidate *in terms of the criteria* is necessary. Each search committee member should have a copy of the instrument at hand and complete it immediately after the interview.

STRUCTURING THE FORMAL INTERVIEW

Search committees use a variety of techniques to interview candidates. Often there is no plan for questioning interviewees. Each committee member asks his/her own questions without consultation with others. Other search committees draw up a list of questions and ask each candidate the same questions.

A recommended procedure is for the search committee to list areas it wishes to explore and pose topics on which a candidate can express him/herself.

FORMAL INTERVIEW QUESTION DEVELOPMENT

A highly successful method of developing appropriate questions comes from a careful analysis of the position and the development of questions about the experiences the candidate has had that relate to the position requirements. The candidate responds as to how he/she meets each requirement or how he/she has behaved in the past when dealing with such requirements. If the basic question is well phrased, the candidate's response should lead to additional questions about the basic requirements.

One interesting method for developing questions is called "Behavior Description Interviewing." "The behavior description interview proceeds by a structured pattern of questions designed to probe the applicant's past behavior in specific situations."* Basically, the procedure involves analyzing a position, listing the position requirements, and developing a series of probes into how a candidate has behaved in situations related to the position. The argument is that past behavior is the best predictor of future behavior.

Some examples of interview question development follow:

INTERVIEW QUESTION DEVELOPMENT

Position: Admissions Counselor (a relatively junior position often filled by a person for whom it will be a

---

*Janz, Tom, Hillervik, Lowell and Gilmore, David C. (1986) *Behavior Descriptive Interviewing*. Boston: Allyn & Bacon, p.3.

first full-time position. Previous related behavior questions may be more difficult to formulate for a person new to the work force)

Requirements:

1. Ability to show potential students how college will fit their plans for schooling and careers.

2. Must be perceived as helpful, concerned and interested in potential student.

3. Must be able to provide a glimpse into student life at the college.

4. Presents the college at high schools, college fairs and community colleges.

5. Dresses appropriately.

6. Team worker—cooperative.

7. Works evenings and travels frequently.

8. Maintains detailed written records.

Interview:

After an interviewer explains the nature of the position and the duties, the following areas are probed:

Questions:

1. Admissions counseling basically is convincing qualified persons that Black Rock University will meet their educational and professional needs. What have you done in the past that is similar?

2. (a) Describe activities in which you are involved that are aimed at helping, reassuring or advising people?

(b) In your own college career did you ever convince a fellow student that he/she should not drop out? How did you do this? What were the results of your efforts?

3. How will you portray college student life to high school seniors? What do you think are the most important aspects to stress? Why?

4. (a) What methods will you develop for contacting prospective students other than the traditional routes? Where will you go to find students of the kind that usually enroll in Black Rock University?

(b) What experience have you had at college admissions fairs? Whom did you see and what did you do?

5. (a) How do you dress on different occasions? Where do you feel casual dress is appropriate in the work place? How did you dress in your last position?

(b) Has anyone ever criticized how you dress? how did you handle that criticism?

6. (a) Tell us about experiences you have had working with groups and individuals from various ages and ethnic backgrounds.

(b) What was the most trying time you ever had with a co-worker? How did you handle it? How was it resolved?

7. (a) How would you describe your work habits? Describe any work experience you had that involved extensive travel.

(b) Did you ever feel that you were being exploited by working overtime or odd hours? How did you handle that situation?

8. When have you had to maintain detailed records. What kind were they and how useful were these records to you later?

INTERVIEW QUESTION DEVELOPMENT
Position: Assistant/Associate Professor—Sociology

Requirements:

1. Thorough knowledge of basic literature.
2. Specialized knowledge in area of demography and religion.
3. Ability to motivate and direct undergraduate and graduate students.
4. Contributions to various college-wide studies and committees.
5. Acts as advisor to Sociology Club.
6. Has a record of significant research.
7. Has made a contribution to the literature (publications).

Interview Questions:

1. In your field, which writers have influenced you the most and how do you think that this is displayed in your teaching and research. (The answer should suggest further questions in this area.)
2. What issues in demography and religion interest you the most and what contributions to the field are you making or plan to make?

3. Give some examples of how you helped students develop a deep interest in Sociology. Explain what techniques you used.
4. Discuss the committees on which you have served and the impact these committees' reports have had on the university.
5. Discuss your service with student groups and the activities you had the most influence implementing.

INTERVIEW QUESTION DEVELOPMENT
Position: Dean, School of Arts and Sciences

Requirements:
1. Lead Curriculum Development.
2. Recommend faculty members for hiring, promotion and tenure.
3. Encourage grants application.
4. Encourage scholarly activity.
5. Promote shared governance.

Interview Questions:
1. What are your achievements in curriculum development and what means did you use to accomplish them?
2. Provide some examples of how you decided to recommend promotions and tenure. Also Discuss the times you did not make such recommendations.
3. How have you been effective in encouraging grants applications? What strategies did you employ?
4. What are some examples of resisting faculty or peer pressure for taking actions that you did not want to take?
5. Are there some examples you can provide where people resisted your efforts or policies and later were convinced of the correctness of your position?
6. Of which achievements as a manager are you most proud?
7. What is the worst administrative mistake you ever made? If the same situation arose again, how would you handle it?
8. Give some examples of how you behaved when a superior enforced a policy with which you disagreed.

9. Describe how you have handled disputes between faculty members, between faculty groups, or between a faculty member and a student.
10. Given limited financial resources, what system of rewards would you put in place to encourage scholarship?
11. Give examples of how you worked with faculty groups to solve problems of common concern.

SEARCH COMMITTEE FORMAL INTERVIEW SEQUENCE

The formal interview must be carefully structured. It has a number of important elements:

1. Search committee members are fully briefed. They know the candidates' formal qualifications and accomplishments; they have letters of recommendation and reports of telephone conversations with referees and candidates; they have seen the candidates' transcripts. The search committee members have agreed on areas to cover in the interview and, in some cases, have assigned specific lines of inquiry to particular members. All committee members are fully aware of lines of inquiry which are inappropriate.

2. The candidate has an itinerary and some notification of campus issues which the successful candidate may face. The candidate enters the formal meeting *after* having had informal meetings. He/she has some understanding of the problems and issues at the college.

   The candidate fully understands how his/her expenses are to be handled.

3. The chairperson and search committee members greet the candidate when he/she is brought to the interview site. The candidate is given evidence that the committee is friendly and approves of him/her. Hands are shaken; members smile; eye contact is established when greetings are exchanged and later, when questions are asked.

4. The opening consists of small talk and inconsequential but friendly "pitter patter." (There is some evidence to show that such social interaction is necessary before getting to basic issues.) The opening lasts five to seven minutes but the search committee members do not begin conversations among themselves as that may hinder the formal beginnings of the interview.

5. The chairperson opens the formal part of the interview ensuring that each committee member is given his/her opportunity to ask questions. If any important question or issues (discussed in planning meetings) are unasked, the chairperson eventually poses the question.

6. When committee members have asked all the questions needed, the chairperson then asks the candidate if he/she has any questions.

This question to the candidate is not just to signal the pending termination of the interview (it is that, too). By now the candidate should have developed a number of questions raised in the informal or semi-formal meetings. His/her own investigations prior to arrival on campus also might have raised some issues. To some extent, the quality of the candidate's questions may indicate how serious a candidate he/she is.

Usually, search committee members should not respond to questions about salary or benefits. Such questions should be discussed with the personnel officer or the person who is authorized to make an offer.

INTERVIEWS WITH ADMINISTRATORS

Depending on the wishes of the various administrators involved, interviews with them should be scheduled after the search committee interview with the candidate. Deans of academic instructional units usually want to see candidates. In some colleges vice-presidents and even presidents may wish to interview candidates. Often a search committee will not present a candidate to an administrator unless the committee intends to recommend him/her.

The administrator interview is conducted with the knowledge that the search committee is fully confident about the subject matter knowledge of applicants for teaching/research positions and reasonably confident about the candidates for other posts. Normally, the administrator does not probe into discipline knowledge but deals with ideas, human interaction skills, college structure, and duties over and above teaching. The administrator looks for motivation, energy level, resolve and appearance.

As the interviews with administrators usually takes place towards the end of the on-campus visit, an administrator may question the candidate about how the candidate interprets what he/she observed during the day.

Sometimes, for major positions, the president and his/her cabinet may interview candidates for the purpose of deciding what that person will add to the strengths of the institution. Much of these discussions revolve around the administrative "style" for administrative positions. The senior officials may try to detect potential allies or rivals in candidates.

EXIT INTERVIEWS

A number of colleges have tried to protect themselves from complaints by conducting exit interviews. These are brief.

In one kind of exit interview the Affirmative Action Officer asks the candidate to complete a form indicating that he/she is satisfied that there has been no discriminatory remark or action during the interview process. The manner in which this is done must be most careful for such an interview could be perceived as intimidating. Several Affirmative Action Officers report that complaints about questions on race, religion, national origin or handicap are rare. The report is that the most common complaint is from women who believe that they have been patronized when asked questions about child care or how their husbands felt about their working. Such questions generally are not lawful and are to be avoided.

It is also usual to schedule an interview with the person authorized to make an offer, where such matters as a definite salary or salary range and benefits may be discussed.

The candidate then is returned to his hotel, airport or other convenient place by a member of the search committee.

An indication should be given to the candidate as to when he/she should receive notification of the disposition of his/her candidacy.

BLACK ROCK UNIVERSITY
Candidate Exit Interview

NAME _____

ADDRESS _____
                                    City, state , zip code

Position Applied For _____

1. Were you at any time given the impression that the interview was a sham or less than honest?
   Yes _____ No _____ (If yes, explain)

2. Were you made comfortable, and was an effort made by the interviewer(s) to make you feel relaxed?
   Yes _____ No _____ (If no, explain)

3. Did you feel intimidated at any time?
   Yes _____ No _____ (If yes, explain)

4. Overall, did you feel that it was a fair and equitable interview and that you received due consideration for the job?
   Yes _____ No _____ (If yes, explain)

5. Other comments _____
   _____

   Signature of Applicant _____
   Signature of EEO Officer _____
                              Date _____

LEGAL CONCERNS

Discriminatory Questions

Persons taking part in interviews of candidates should familiarize themselves with the position description and with the qualifications required. This will help ensure that questions asked in the course of interviews are directly related to the position.

Questions unrelated to the position may be perceived as discriminatory and lead to litigation. Thus, questions about a candidate's education, licensure, scholarship and experience, as well as future research plans and possible publications, are appropriate. On the other hand, queries about age, religion, handicap, race, color, sex, national origin, marital status, birth control methods, or arrangements for child care generally are not directly related to the position description and qualifications. They are inappropriate and often unlawful.

Exception for Religious Institutions

A religious corporation or church-related institution may wish to have all or a preponderance of its faculty and staff reflect its religious preference. Where this is the case, the religious institution should review with its legal counsel whether it qualifies for an exception, and what would be deemed lawful questions about religion to ask candidates. Legal counsel also will help evaluate possible risks of loss of public funds.

Sex as a BFOQ

Where sex is a bona fide occupational qualification (BFOQ), as it would be for a position as a wet nurse, it is lawful to consider only persons from one sex as applicants.

Sexual Harassment

Search Committee members should understand what constitutes sexual harassment of females and males and avoid any appearance of harassment. Sexual harassment involves situations where employment benefits depend upon a person's submission to unwanted sexual advances, or where sexual harassment creates a working environment that is hostile and intimidating. Both males and females are protected from sexual harassment. Employers are expected to investigate complaints and deal effectively with harassment.

Loss of Public Funding

Unlawful discriminatory interviewing may place at risk an institution's federal or state financial funding and/or may result in an award of money damages making whole the applicant who suffered discrimination.

Chapter VI

Making the Recommendation and the Offer

ONE CANDIDATE

If the college policy is to interview one person at a time and decide on that candidate's suitability immediately after the campus visit, the process of deciding is relatively simple. The chairperson of the search committee collects all the recommendations and evaluations and places them before the committee. The question to answer is simple—"Is this person suitable for the position or not?"

The search committee reviews all the materials and tries to arrive at a consensus. Unless there is a solid measure of support for the candidate, it is unwise to make a recommendation. In such a case, the search committee must bring in the next candidate on the list.

If a candidate is suitable for the position, the chairperson of the search committee composes a memorandum to the supervisor indicating that the committee is recommending the candidate.

SEVERAL CANDIDATES

If a number of candidates have been interviewed, the formulation of a recommendation may be more difficult. Many opinions and observations must be taken into consideration. If several names are to be submitted to a supervisor, it must be determined whether the person to whom the names will be submitted wishes the candidates to be ranked in order of attractiveness or suitability. Often, if the position is for a major administrative office, the president, vice president or other college official may wish to have three to five names from which to chose.

Presumably, the official who will make the final selection has met with the various candidates and will be able to measure his/her own reactions against those of the search committee.

The chairperson of the search committee should assemble all the materials that have been returned from the various persons, committees and groups with which the candidates have met.

If the search committee wishes, there may be a numerical value attached to each of the observation or evaluation sheets. This may be valuable only if each of the candidates has met the same people while on campus. Otherwise, scoring will not have any credibility.

The search committee must review all the information which it has received. In some cases, it may be necessary to contact persons who made comments which the committee does not understand or that need further clarification.

The search committee should refer again to the search criteria and also come to some agreement on other qualities that have come to light about each candidate while he/she was on campus. As the process goes forward, one or more candidates should emerge as the most attractive.

Once the search committee has arrived at a consensus, a formal memorandum is sent to the supervisor.

MAKING THE OFFER

When the supervisor has received the recommendation of the search committee and agrees with it, he/she usually telephones the recommended candidate for a final discussion of salary, rank, and other conditions of the position. Such matters as moving expenses are also part of the offer.

While there is little if any documentation, it is widely believed that all offers should be subject to negotiation. However, if a system has allocated an exact amount of money and the conditions are firm, that should be stated to the candidate at the time of the offer.

Some candidates will accept an offer at the time it is made. Others will ask for a week or two to decide, citing the need to dicuss the matter with a spouse and check out local living conditions.

Occasionally, a candidate will ask for an unusually long period in which to consider the offer. If this occurs, there should be a deadline given. If the candidate has not replied by the deadline date, he/she should be sent a letter informing him/her that the offer no longer exists.

If a candidate refuses the offer or does not reply within the agreed-upon time frame, the second candidate on the list should be contacted. This should continue until a candidate has accepted the offer. If there are no other acceptable candidates, the Search is usually re-opened, much to the chagrin of many parties.

Letter of Appointment — Faculty Member

June 23, 19--

Dr. Daniel P. Jones
433 Blank Street
Obscure, PA 16900

I am pleased to offer you the position of Assistant Professor, Sociology at step IV of the scale, that is, twenty-four thousand seven hundred dollars (24,700).[1]

Terms and benefits are contained in the Collective Bargaining Agreement, a copy of which your union representative will send to you in due course.[2]

The first day for commencing your duties is September 2, 19--, the date for opening exercises.[3]

This offer will remain open until July 12, 19--. Please let me have your written response to this offer by that date.[4]

Sincerely,

James R. Roils
Dean of Social Sciences

Important Elements in Letter

(1) Offer of rank, salary and step made.
(2) Benefits, length of academic year, promotion policy, grievance procedures, other terms of employment are covered in Collective Bargaining agreement with faculty union.
(3) Starting date noted.
(4) Response must be made to offer by specified date.

May 12, 19--

Dr. Henrietta P. Grand
Apt. 4, 18 Cedar Street
Carmel, KY 40400

Dear Dr. Grand:

I am pleased to offer you the position of Dean of the College of Education at Black Rock University. We are prepared to offer you an annual salary of fifty thousand dollars ($50,000).[1]

As we discussed, the position carries a tenured professorship and would begin July 1, 19--. Other conditions of employment are outlined in the Administrative Handbook, a copy of which is enclosed.[2]

We also agreed that the University would allow you up to five thousand dollars ($5,000) for moving expenses. (You will need to keep receipts for expenditures for moving.)[3]

The starting date for taking up your duties is July 1, 19--.[3]

Please let me have your written acceptance of this offer before June 5, 19--.[4]

Sincerely,

Henry B. Green
President

Important Elements in Letter

(1) Offer of position and salary made.

(2) Benefits and conditions enclosed in document.

(3) Moving expenses noted.

(4) Written acceptance required.

LEGAL CONCERNS

Defamation

When the search committee members reach the point where they must discuss and vote on candidates and make recommendations, they should take special care to carry out these activities in a completely businesslike manner.

Remarks about candidates made by search committee members within the proper confines of such a meeting generally will be accorded a qualified privilege protecting against claims of defamation of character, even where an untrue statement may have been made. A qualified privilege will not stand, however, where untrue remarks are made outside a proper meeting, such as at a party or on the golf course or where such remarks clearly are malicious.

Thus, it is critical that search committee members and relevant others understand their roles and act responsibly.

Court Order to Reveal Vote

Members of search committees should take special care to make recommendations and vote only on the basis of a candidate's professional qualifications. Then, should charges of discrimination lead to a court's ordering individual members to reveal their votes, each member will be prepared to justify his/her vote by referring to the candidate's professional qualifications, disproving any allegations that the vote was based on discriminatory reasons, such as race, sex, age, handicap, religion, color or national origin.

Offer Misunderstood

As for making an offer to a candidate, a duly authorized person who makes an offer of employment to a candidate must keep in mind that he/she is part of the process of creating a legally binding agreement between the institution and the individual.

The terms and conditions of employment should be discussed thoroughly so that there is mutual understanding of exactly what the offer is. In general, it is wise to put an offer in writing and to require a written acceptance.

A written offer should include, at a minimum, a brief description of the job, a statement of the salary, and the dates of the term of appointment.

Ineffective Withdrawal

Where an offer or acceptance must be withdrawn, it should be done in a timely fashion and should be in writing.

Chapter VII

Cautions and Concerns

There are a number of areas which are of special concern to search committees. Each committee should be aware of these sensitive issues which may arise.

LACK OF CONFIDENTIALITY AND OPEN MEETING LAWS

Much has been written lately about the "sunshine" or "open meeting" laws in several states. These laws provide that the public must have access to information and meetings where public decisions are made. Open meeting laws generally do not apply to private institutions. Such laws make it possible that finalists—those to be interviewed for positions—may have their names made public before a decision about the person to be employed has been made.

State supported institutions in several states must make known the names of persons being seriously considered for positions. The media has been known to publish the names of persons who are being considered for positions, from professors to presidents. For instance, many persons refuse to be considered for positions in the State of Florida for fear of being embarrassed, should their home institutions find out that they are being considered for a position at another institution. Not only do candidates not want their interest in leaving their home campus known (for many legitimate reasons), but their chagrin when they are known to be "losers" may be even more humiliating when they return to campus "unsuccessful" in their bid for another position.

There is little a college search committee can do about confidentiality if the state laws dictate that information about candidates is to be open to the public. However, search committees have been known to be careless and have revealed information that was not decreed by law.

Several years ago, a state official was interviewed for a position as a dean at a state college in the same state where he had some supervisory duties (as a State Department of Education Official) over state college curricula. The search committee knew that the candidate was involved in a decision about changing the requirements for teacher education in the state. A number of members of the search committee were opposed to the proposed new requirements and drew the candidate into a discussion of the new proposals. As reported throughout the state college system, there was a "heated discussion" between some committee members and the candidate. The candidate was not successful but the story was reported widely. Such a breach of confidentiality on the part of the search committee can hardly inspire future applicants to apply for positions at that college.

Search committee members receive many confidential pieces of information about applicants and candidates. Referees will report on an individual's marital problems, financial difficulties, role in in-fighting in campus politics and many other highly personal matters. While they do not do this in written documents as a rule, there may be notes of telephone calls reporting this information in the files and a search committee member may report it to the committee as a whole. If this occurs, committee members have an ethical duty to keep all this information in confidence.

CONFLICT OF INTEREST

The possibility of an inappropriate person being selected as a member of a search committee has been mentioned. However, sometimes search committees will be formed and decisions made before the supervisor is aware of what is happening, and this can have most unpleasant results.

In one Pennsylvania university an acting chairperson of an academic department moved very rapidly towards the appointment of a temporary lecturer. In fact, he was at the point of interviewing candidates when the supervisor discovered that the search committee was moving faster than the supervisor had anticipated. The acting chairperson did not inform his supervisor that he had appointed his search committee, nor did he inform the dean as to who the search committee members were. As it turned out there were two final candidates for the position. Each one was the spouse of a member of the search committee. The dean insisted that the search committee be reconstructed with no members on it who had obvious conflicts of interest. However, the president then returned from a trip and discovered the situation. The president was so incensed that the search was abolished, and the position for which the search was opened was also abolished.

84

Search committee members should not be related by kinship or strong personal friendship ties to persons who will apply for the positions open. Violating this primary rule is an invitation for serious trouble.

Persons who are known adversaries of applicants likewise should not be members of a search committee. It is incumbent on a search committee member to disqualify him/herself when such a conflict arises, or the committee chairperson must do it.

WRITTEN COMMUNICATIONS

One of the most frequent mistakes made by search committees is the use of very poorly formatted or written communications that go out to applicants and candidates.

The most gross error in replying to candidates has already been mentioned—that is, acknowledging an application by post card. Post cards are not designed to be the carriers of confidential information. Some institutions continue to make this error in judgment. In 1985, a small college in the Chicago area acknowledged applications for the presidency by post card much to the indignation of many applicants.

Many colleges still acknowledge applicants by using printed forms. Sometimes these forms make some attempt at disguising the fact that they are forms. They fail, however, when the form has been duplicated, and a name and address is typed in using a different type style. A number of colleges add insult to injury when they misspell the name of the applicant to whom they are replying.

Some colleges send letters which appear to be originals by reason of clever use of memory or automatic typewriters or word processors. Then they give up the pretense of sending an individual letter by having spaces to check off in the text of the letter. For example:

We have received your application. Please have the following materials sent to us by June 5:

Transcripts	_____
Personal Statement	_____
Four letters of reference	_____

An "X" is placed in the space next to the item(s) the search committee wishes to receive.

There is little reason for such discourtesies in the day when even the smallest and most obscure college has access to modern word processing equipment. It is also doubtful that the time it takes to send out businesslike letters is actually less than it takes to send out letters that do not represent the college well.

When an applicant receives one of the types of post cards or letters described above, there is always a suspicion that a clerk is actually making the decisions about the manner in which correspondence is carried on or that the search is being conducted by persons of poor judgment.

INTERVIEWING

A number of problems may arise with interviewing. Aside from the use of obviously biased remarks discussed previously, search committees have been known to conduct interviews *before* the date for the cut off of applications. Inexperienced and poorly supervised committees have been known to become so enthusiastic about a candidate that they will schedule an interview before all applications are in. A few of these search committees have even recommended candidates for positions before that date.

A serious applicant who finds out that the rules of the game, including the closing date as laid down by the college's advertisement, have not been followed might complain. The responsible college officer may have to vacate the search and the process will have to begin again.

TELEPHONE CALLS

College search committee members have been known to make telephone calls that can cause a candidate severe discomfort. Consider the vice president of a small college who was seeking another position and did not want it known in her own college. One day she arrived to find a note that said, "Marty Jones called and wants to know if you are still interested in the presidency of College X. Please call her back." The message was left at the switchboard. There is little hope that this vice president's search for another position is a secret any longer and that the caller—a member of the search committee—has violated confidentiality.

INTERNAL COMMUNICATION

All members of a search team must know the rules of the search. This goes for the secretarial and clerical assistants too. They must understand the various kinds of communication, the necessity for confidentiality, the need to be discrete with telephone calls, and the purpose of the various activities in which the search committee is engaging. Secretarial and clerical assistants should be briefed regularly by the search committee chair and, at the outset, by the supervisor.

CONCLUSIONS

This publication has not and could not detail all the mistakes that human beings are capable of making when searching for college personnel. The cautions noted are the result of discussions with many position seekers who have been dismayed with the actions or apparent actions of colleges searching for personnel. They point to a need for colleges "to get their act together" when searching. With adequate consideration and care, successful searches can be conducted in a manner that will be a credit to all parties.

Appendix I

Resources for Legal Information in Secondary and Higher Education

If you have found the information contained in this monograph to be helpful in your day-to-day operations and as a reference it is quite likely that you may also be interested in other titles included in the *The Higher Education Administration Series* or in our publications that offer quarterly updates on case law related to various fields of education.

At the back of this book is a form for ordering other titles available from College Administration Publications. When you place your order you may wish to copy the form rather than tearing out the page.

Other titles in *The Higher Education Administration Series:*
► Administering College and University Housing:
  A Legal Perspective
► The Dismissal of Students with Mental Disorders:
  Legal Issues, Policy Considerations
  and Alternative Responses
► Computers in Education:
  Legal Liabilities and Ethical Issues
  Concerning Their Use and Misuse
► A Practical Guide to Legal Issues Affecting Teachers
► Faculty / Staff Nonrenewal and Dismissal for Cause
  in Institutions of Higher Education

The following publications offer the reader a quarterly report on recent precedent setting higher court decisions covering a wide range of subjects in the area encompassed by the self-descriptive title. In addition, through the accumulated back issues, and in the "College" publications, a casebook, each of these publications are also excellent comprehensive references that can be of great help in day-to-day operations and long range planning:
► The College Student and the Courts
► The College Administrator and the Courts
► The Schools and the Courts
  While primarily written for practicing administrators, superintendents, school boards, teachers and legal counsel in secondary education, this publication is of great value to related schools of education.

Order Blank

Bill to:.............................   *Ship to:*.............................

....

....

Quantity	*Item & Price*	*Total*

MONOGRAPHS

_____ **The Dismissal of Students with Mental Disorders:** _____
1 to 9 copies @ $9.95; 10 or more copies @ $9.50

_____ **Administering College and University Housing:** _____
1 to 9 copies @ $9.95; 10 or more copies @ $9.50

_____ **A Practical Guide to Legal Issues Affecting
College Teachers** _____
1 to 9 copies @ $4.95; 10 to 24 copies @ $3.95;
25 or more copies @ $3.50

_____ **Computers in Education: Legal Liabilities and
Ethical Issues Concerning Their Use and Misuse** _____
1 to 9 copies @ $9.95; 10 or more copies @ $9.50

_____ **Faculty / Staff Nonrenewal and Dismissal for Cause
in Institutions of Higher Education** _____
1 to 9 copies @ $9.95; 10 or more copies @ $9.50

_____ **A Guide to Successful Searches for College Personnel:
Policies, Procedures, and Legal Issues** _____
1 to 9 copies @ $9.95; 10 or more copies @ $9.50

PERIODICALS

_____ **The College Student and the Courts**
Includes casebook, all back issues and four
quarterly updating supplements.............$98.50 _____

_____ **The College Administrator and the Courts**
Includes casebook, all back issues and four
quarterly updating supplements.............$77.50 _____

_____ **The Schools and the Courts**
Includes over 600 pages of back issues and four
updating reports..........................$67.50 _____

*Postage (if payment accompanies
order we will ship postpaid)* _____

North Carolina residents add appropriate sales tax _____

Total _____

Address Orders to:
College Administration Publications, Inc.
Dept. SS, P.O. Box 8492, Asheville, NC 28814

☐ Pricing of the above publications was correct on the publication
date of this monograph. If you wish to be advised of current prices
of titles you have ordered before shipment, please check.

☐ For further information regarding any of the above titles please
indicate with check here and in the quantity column of each publication and we will forward current brochures and information.